M000099095

JEFFERSON PILOT
FINANCIAL

1903 ◆ 2003

A Century of Excellence

JEFFREY L. RODENGEN & RICHARD F. HUBBARD

JEFFERSON PILOT
FINANCIAL
1903 ◆ 2003
A Century of Excellence

JEFFREY L. RODENGEN & RICHARD F. HUBBARD

Edited by Jon VanZile
Design and layout by Dennis Shockley

For Captain Aubrey Goodwin—always my favorite skipper.
—Richard F. Hubbard

WRITE STUFF

Write Stuff Enterprises, Inc.
1001 South Andrews Avenue
Second Floor
Fort Lauderdale, FL 33316
1-800-900-Book (1-800-900-2665)
(954) 462-6657
www.writestuffbooks.com

Copyright © 2003 by Write Stuff Enterprises, Inc. All rights reserved. No part of this book may be reproduced or transmitted in any form by any means, electronic or mechanical, including photocopying and recording, or by any information storage or retrieval system, without permission in writing from the publisher.

Publisher's Cataloging in Publication

Rodengen, Jeffrey L.
 Jefferson Pilot Financial, 1903-2003:
a century of excellence/Jeffrey L. Rodengen &
Richard F. Hubbard; edited by Jon VanZile;
design and layout by Dennis Shockley. – 1st ed.
 p. cm.
 Includes bibliographical references and index.
 LCCN 2002114050
 ISBN 0-945903-99-5

 1. Jefferson-Pilot Life Insurance Company –
History. 2. Jefferson Pilot Financial (Firm) –
History. 3. Insurance companies – United States
– History. I. Hubbard, Richard F. II. Title.

 HG8963.J442R63 2003   368.32'006573
                        QBI03-200365

Library of Congress
Catalog Card Number 2002114050

ISBN 0-945903-99-5

Completely produced in the
United States of America
10 9 8 7 6 5 4 3 2 1

Also by Jeffrey L. Rodengen

The Legend of Chris-Craft

IRON FIST: The Lives of Carl Kiekhaefer

Evinrude-Johnson and The Legend of OMC

Serving the Silent Service: The Legend of Electric Boat

The Legend of Dr Pepper/Seven-Up

The Legend of Honeywell

The Legend of Briggs & Stratton

The Legend of Ingersoll-Rand

The Legend of Stanley: 150 Years of The Stanley Works

The MicroAge Way

The Legend of Halliburton

The Legend of York International

The Legend of Nucor Corporation

The Legend of Goodyear: The First 100 Years

The Legend of AMP

The Legend of Cessna

The Legend of VF Corporation

The Spirit of AMD

The Legend of Rowan

New Horizons: The Story of Ashland Inc.

The History of American Standard

The Legend of Mercury Marine

The Legend of Federal-Mogul

Against the Odds: Inter-Tel—The First 30 Years

State of the Heart: The Practical Guide to Your Heart and Heart Surgery
with Larry W. Stephenson, M.D.

The Legend of Pfizer

The Legend of Worthington Industries

The Legend of Trinity Industries, Inc.

The Legend of IBP, Inc.

The Legend of Cornelius Vanderbilt Whitney

The Legend of Amdahl

The Legend of Litton Industries

The Legend of Gulfstream

The Legend of Bertram
with David A. Patten

The Legend of Ritchie Bros. Auctioneers

The Legend of ALLTEL
with David A. Patten

The Yes, you can of Invacare Corporation
with Anthony L. Wall

The Ship in the Balloon: The Story of Boston Scientific and the Development of Less-Invasive Medicine

The Legend of Day & Zimmermann

The Legend of Noble Drilling

Fifty Years of Innovation: Kulicke & Soffa

Biomet—From Warsaw to the World
with Richard F. Hubbard

NRA: An American Legend

The Heritage and Values of RPM, Inc.

The Marmon Group: The First Fifty Years

The Legend of Grainger

The Legend of The Titan Corporation
with Richard F. Hubbard

The Legend of Discount Tire
with Richard F. Hubbard

The Legend of La-Z-Boy
with Richard F. Hubbard

The Legend of McCarthy
with Richard F. Hubbard

TABLE OF CONTENTS

Introduction vi

Acknowledgments viii

Chapter I   Rock Ribbed and Ancient 10

Chapter II   A World of Change 34

Chapter III   Into the Modern Age 62

Chapter IV   A Wise Investment 92

Chapter V   JP Rising 106

Chapter VI   A Market Leader 120

Notes to Sources 144

Index 150

INTRODUCTION

OLD-TIMERS OFTEN talk about Jefferson-Pilot as if it were actually three distinct companies, each an era in a century-long history of growth and success.

The first of these companies dates to the turn-of-the-century countryside in North Carolina. Things were different back then: The South was still feeling the aftershocks of the Civil War, and the United States stood on the brink of a rapid technological and social evolution. In 1903, in Kitty Hawk, North Carolina, humanity slipped the bonds of gravity for the first time when Wilbur and Orville Wright's flying machine achieved successful flight. It was an apt beginning for a remarkable century.

That same year Southern Loan & Trust (later Pilot Life) sold its first life insurance policy, surely one of the first sold in the state of North Carolina by a local company. The sale would later be identified as the founding of Jefferson Pilot Financial. A few years later, a neighboring company, Jefferson Standard, sold its first life insurance policy.

By virtue of time and place, Jefferson Standard and Pilot Life had more in common than they did in contrast. Both operated from Greensboro, and both were founded as purely southern institutions. Their policies were aimed at locals, and their investments poured through the economy of their home state.

The companies also shared a legacy of strong leadership. At Pilot Life, President A. W. McAlister imprinted his personality on every detail, even down to the window glass installed in Sedgefield, the company's gracious rural headquarters outside Greensboro. A health advocate, McAlister believed that the ultravoilet rays in sunlight were beneficial and bought special window glass that let the sun beam in. A firm moralist, shrewd marketer, and corporate citizen, McAlister pushed Pilot Life to diversify beyond life insurance into a variety of financial products.

Jefferson Standard, meanwhile, prospered under the guidance of Julian Price, who assumed the presidency in 1919 and would later be regarded as the architect of the modern Jefferson-Pilot Corporation. Price's broad expertise included sales, marketing, investments, and even acquisition. It was Price who directed Jefferson Standard to buy a majority interest in Pilot Life and Price who expanded Jefferson Standard beyond insurance. In the late 1920s, urged by Price's son-in-law Joseph M. Bryan, Jefferson Standard purchased a radio station, founding Jefferson Standard Broadcasting. The subsidiary grew steadily, adding new signals and television stations and even expanding into event production.

Later, as the last official act of his leadership, Price organized a complicated, three-way transaction that merged Pilot Life with another local company, Gate City Life Insurance, then placed both under the ownership of Jefferson Standard. With Price's retirement in 1947, the first era in Jefferson-Pilot's history drew to a close.

The second era began in the post–World War II era. American industry and technology were spreading around the globe even as the country went through wrenching periods of social growth. Jefferson Standard and Pilot Life faced these triumphant and trying years together, under a series of leaders that included Howard Holderness, O. F. Stafford, Louis Stephens, and Roger Soles.

With its downtown headquarters in Greensboro's tallest building, Jefferson Standard was a pure-play life insurance company with a strong securities and investment operation. It was a conservative company—conservatively dressed, managed, and advertised.

Pilot Life, in contrast, was a multiline company with a much more folksy, high-profile image. "The Pilot" offered group, home service, scholastic, and even group health and disability insurance. Quick to see the potential in television advertising, Pilot Life sponsored Atlantic Coast Conference (ACC) basketball in the 1950s, making itself one of the most recognized insurance companies in the South. The company's jingle, "Sail With the Pilot," became popular at high school and college events.

Jefferson Standard and Pilot Life grew as the insurance industry changed. Universal life insurance was introduced in the late 1970s. In the 1980s, life insurance companies suffered through a protracted real estate downturn and risky investments in junk bonds. Fortunately, Jefferson Standard and Pilot Life prospered through these changes, drawing upon wise investments and decades of expertise.

By 1987, however, Jefferson Standard CEO Roger Soles recognized it was time for a change. He saw that because of the increasing power of technology and the growing burden of taxation, Jefferson Standard and Pilot Life would do better as a united organization than as two distinct companies. That year, the companies merged, signaling the end of the second era of Jefferson-Pilot's history.

In the early 1990s, the board of directors began a search to replace Roger Soles, who planned to retire in 1993. David Stonecipher was named president and chief executive officer, the first outsider to assume the top post, and he brought ambitious plans. In his first 18 months, Stonecipher assembled a management team to shake up Jefferson-Pilot and put the company's considerable capital to more aggressive use.

The effect of the Stonecipher team was electrifying. Sales and marketing efforts were energized as the company rapidly created new distribution channels. Meanwhile, a newly formed mergers and acquisitions group was busy looking for opportunities. It didn't take long. Between 1995 and 1999, Jefferson-Pilot negotiated a string of transformative acquisitions, including Kentucky Central Life, Alexander Hamilton, Chubb Life, and Guarantee Life

These acquisitions kicked off the third era of the company's first century. Through the acquisition of new companies, Jefferson-Pilot picked up new and important products and dramatically increased its distribution channels. It transitioned from a regional, primarily southern company to a national leader in its industry in terms of insurance in force, shareholder return, and revenue.

In 2000, hoping to maintain its momentum, Jefferson-Pilot leaders announced the Premier Partnering strategy, designed to recruit top-producing agents and double life insurance sales in two years. These were ambitious goals, to be sure, but Jefferson-Pilot's record had silenced doubters.

As the company prepared for its centennial in 2003, Jefferson-Pilot employees could take a great deal of pride and satisfaction in their company—whichever of the various Jefferson-Pilot families they happened to work for in the past. A *Fortune* 500 company, Jefferson-Pilot was important for reasons that went beyond its balance sheet. Through its investments, it had participated in the transformation of the South. And through its products, it had funneled tens of millions of dollars to people in their times of greatest need. As one Jefferson-Pilot agent observed, at the time of death, the life insurance agent is often the only person to show up on the doorstep with relief.

In 2003, with the company on the threshold of its next century, one thing is certain: Its position is forever secure in the history of its home state, the lives it has touched, and the industry it has helped lead.

ACKNOWLEDGMENTS

A GREAT NUMBER OF PEOPLE assisted in the research, preparation, and publication of *Jefferson Pilot Financial: A Century of Excellence.*

This book would not have been possible if not for the skill and perseverance of our researchers, Jerry Adams and Sheridan Hill. Their exhaustive survey of Jefferson-Pilot's archives laid a solid foundation on which to build the book. Jon VanZile, executive editor, oversaw the text and photos from beginning to end, and Dennis Shockley, art director, brought the story to life with his keen eye for design.

We are especially indebted to company executives at Jefferson-Pilot who freely gave their time and insight to the project. These include Chairman and CEO David Stonecipher; Vice Chairman and President-Life Companies Ken Mlekush; President and Chief Operating Officer Dennis Glass; Chief Financial Officer and President-Jefferson-Pilot Communications Terry Stone; Executive Vice President and General Counsel John Hopkins; Executive Vice President-Marketing and Distribution Warren May; President-Benefit Partners Bob Bates; Executive Vice President-Underwriting/New Business and Chief Information Officer Chuck

Cornelio; Executive Vice President-Product/Financial Management Mark Konen; Senior Vice President and Chief Investment Officer John Ingram; Senior Vice President-Human Resources Hoyt Phillips; Senior Vice President-General Agency and Chairman and CEO-JPSC Ron Angarella; Senior Vice President-Corporate Development John Still; and Senior Vice President-Marketing Bill Seawell II.

Special gratitude is also owed to Roger Soles, former President and Chief Executive Officer of Jefferson-Pilot Corporation, and Louis Stephens, former President of Pilot Life Insurance, both of whom contributed their memories to the book.

This book benefited greatly from the support of strong advocates at Jefferson-Pilot who freely gave of their time and expertise to make it a reality. Nancy Elkins worked innumerable hours to locate files, photos, and a century's worth of documents to make this project a success.

Many other Jefferson-Pilot executives, employees, retirees, friends, and family members enriched the book by discussing their experiences and lending valued photos from their personal collections.

ACKNOWLEDGMENTS

The authors extend their personal gratitude to Ron Agel, Dick Andrews, Dorothy Austell, Bernie Bernstein, Jim Blackburn, Clarke Brown, Archie Coleman, Sam Cornwell, Loretta Courson, Ann Dowd, Bert East, Sam Elkins, Norm Feinstein, J. J. Field, Joe Freeman, Lloyd Gordon, Guy Hatcher, Ed Hull, Bette B. Johnson, Robert H. Koonts, Bessie Land, Michael Lyman, Randy Macon, Seth Macon, Bob Martin, Craig McIntosh, Jim Melvin, Dave Misiak, Mary Onn Parham, Bill Pickering, Ann Rambeaut, Mary Rambeaut, Bill Seawell Jr., Roger Seigler, Ralph Seigler, John Shreves, Rick Stange, Frank Starr, M.D., Ben Tabor, Molly Walls, Jack Warmath, Joe Webster, Joe Wheeler, and Bill White.

As always, special thanks are extended to the dedicated staff at Write Stuff Enterprises, Inc.: Melody Maysonet, senior editor; Heather Deeley, associate editor; Bonnie Freeman, copyeditor; Sandy Cruz, senior art director; Rachelle Donley and Wendy Iverson, art directors; Mary Aaron, transcriptionist; Barb Koch, indexer; Bruce Borich, production manager; Marianne Roberts, vice president of administration; Sherry Hasso, bookkeeper; Linda Edell, executive assistant to Jeffrey L. Rodengen; Lars Jessen, director of worldwide marketing; Irena Xanthos, manager of sales, promotions, and advertising; Rory Schmer, distribution supervisor; and Jennifer Walter, administrative assistant.

The first life insurance policy written by Southern Loan & Trust, dated 1903. It was a $5,000 policy on the life of Robert Galloway Vaughn.

CHAPTER ONE

ROCK RIBBED AND ANCIENT
1903–1918

A corporation does have a soul, a composite soul as the men who constitute and manage it have. There is no such thing as corporate irresponsibility; a corporation cannot trespass against human rights without some individual or individuals being amenable for it. This is the new corporate conscience.

— A. W. McAlister, President
Southern Life & Trust Company, 1907–1932

IN 1903, AMERICA STOOD poised between its past and its future. In many ways, the United States remained the sparsely populated, agricultural and rural country of its birth. The Civil War, not yet 40 years past, was still fixed in the country's memory, and the lives of most Americans moved to the familiar, comforting rhythms of planting and harvesting.

Yet change was fast approaching. In the five years preceding 1903, America developed a muscular international presence, with military intervention in far-flung places such as Guam, the Philippines, the Caribbean, and the central Pacific. For the first time, average Americans talked about "foreign policy." Even more importantly, scientific innovation was taking off across the country, and more than anything else, this creative impulse would define America's future.

Journalist Mark Sullivan, one of the most respected writers of his age, observed in his landmark 1925 study of America, *In Our Times*, that between 1900 and 1925, society and technology changed faster than at any other time in U.S. history.

In his newspapers of January 1, 1900, the American found no such word as "radio," for that was yet twenty years from coming; nor "movie," for that, too, was still mainly of the future; nor "chauffeur," for the automobile was only just

emerging and had been called "horseless carriage," when treated seriously, but rather more frequently "devil-wagon," and the driver, the "engineer." There was no such word as "aviator"—all that that word implied was still a part of the Arabian Nights.[1]

But the seeds had already been sown for all of these advances. While Ransom E. Olds and Henry Ford worked in Detroit to create the world's largest automobile plant, disparate groups of inventors pursued another of humankind's most enduring dreams: flight. Human flight had been myth and fantasy for centuries, but by the late 1890s, it had become clear that flight was possible. The implications were enormous, too much to even grasp. The idea that a person could use a machine to fly across an ocean seemed otherworldly.

In December 1903, however, in the dunes of coastal North Carolina, two brothers finally broke the bounds of gravity. "Orville and Wilbur Wright were known merely as practical mechanics," Sullivan wrote. "The Wrights had only the resources of a small manufacturing and repair business."[2]

Southern Loan & Trust, which later became Pilot Life, used Pilot Mountain as its logo.

Yet this humble beginning was enough to create and fly the first powered airplane in history. Surprisingly, their inaugural 300-foot flight, which took place on Kill Devil Hills, didn't leave much impression on the public consciousness. It wasn't until 1908 that the *New York Herald* finally broke the story to the world that human flight had been achieved.

Jefferson-Pilot Is Born

The Wright brothers' adopted state was a compelling place. Like the rest of the South, North Carolina was still dealing with echoes of the Civil War and the onrush of the Industrial Revolution. African Americans were moving north in great numbers, attracted to industrial cities like Detroit and wage-paying jobs.

This new focus on industry and technology made America an increasingly sophisticated country, and yet much of the country remained rural, especially in the South. Most of the nation's financial institutions, including banks and insurance companies, were headquartered in the North. Northern agents traveled regularly into warmer climes, seeking to open bank accounts, finance corporations, and offer life and property insurance. But these northern companies weren't always friendly to their southern neighbors, often characterizing the region as disease-infested and socially backward. The American Temperance Life Insurance Company of Hartford added a disclaimer that its life insurance policies would be voided if the insured, without prior consent from the company, dared to visit "those parts of the United States which lie south of Virginia and Kentucky between the first of June and the first of November."[3]

The South, however, would not be dismissed so easily. Throughout the region, there was a growing feeling at the turn of the century that southern institutions should rise to service the local markets. Thus, in 1903, only months before the Wright brothers took off, another event occurred in North Carolina that would have long-lasting repercussions. On July 1, Southern Loan & Trust Company sold its first life insurance policy. The buyer was a 35-year-old North Carolina man. This date would later be designated the official founding of Jefferson-Pilot, a multi-billion-dollar insurance

WHERE THE SOUTHERN LOAN AND TRUST COMPANY
BEGAN BUSINESS IN 1890

and financial services company. By the end of that first day, the company had sold seven policies with a face amount of $16,500.

Southern Loan & Trust was one of a handful of financial companies in the state, and although statewide records do not exist, these life insurance policies were surely among the first sold in North Carolina by a local company.

The Rise of Southern Loan & Trust

Southern Loan & Trust was the offspring of a local real estate company called Worth-Wharton Real Estate & Investment Company. Worth-Wharton had been founded on August 4, 1890, by two Quaker brothers, Dr. John M. Worth and Thomas C. Worth, and Greensboro businessman E. P. Wharton. The firm was initially capitalized with $25,000 and located in the village of Greensboro. An additional $15,000 was paid in the capital stock for a total of $40,000.[4] Although it was primarily

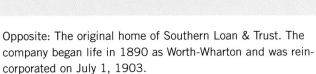

OFFICE OF THE SOUTHERN LOAN AND TRUST COMPANY, 1893-1898

PRESENT HOME AND BANKING-HOUSE OF THE SOUTHERN LOAN AND TRUST COMPANY

Opposite: The original home of Southern Loan & Trust. The company began life in 1890 as Worth-Wharton and was reincorporated on July 1, 1903.

Above: In 1893, Worth-Wharton moved to this larger, two-story brick building in Greensboro. It stood just west of the Guilford County Courthouse, future home of Jefferson Standard.

Above right: In 1899, Worth-Wharton moved again, this time to a five-story building in Greensboro that the local press described as "the most elegant office building between Richmond and Atlanta." It had North Carolina's first working elevator.

a real estate and investment company, it was authorized by charter to sell insurance.[5]

From its first days, Worth-Wharton seemed destined for greatness. Although it started with only one clerk in a 12-foot-by-20-foot office, the company grew quickly, collecting rent, buying and selling real estate, and offering general banking and investment services.[6] As Worth-Wharton grew, the founders organized other insurance companies, including Pilot Fire Insurance Company, the Greensboro Fire Insurance Company, the George Washington Fire Insurance Company, Southern Stock Mutual Fire Insurance Company, and McAlister Underwriters.[7]

In 1893, Worth-Wharton moved to larger headquarters. The two-story building in downtown Greensboro stood on Lawyers' Row, west of the old Guilford County Courthouse at the corner of North Elm and West Market Streets. Six years later, Worth-Wharton moved again, this time to a newly constructed five-story building that one newspaper called "the most elegant office building between Richmond and Atlanta." The new building even had an elevator, the first one in the state of North Carolina. During its open house on New Year's Day 1899, Dick Andrews, a company vice president from the 1960s through 1980s, later wrote, "People

came in horse and buggy from miles around to let their children ride in this new-fangled contraption of the elevator."

Although some businessmen predicted the building was too expensive and too grand for Greensboro, it signaled the city's rise to prominence. In a drugstore across the street, a little-known writer named William Sidney Porter sent out manuscripts under the pen name O. Henry[8] while Lunsford Richardson Sr. mixed chemicals to make batches of the aromatic Vapo-Rub that later launched the Vick Chemical Company.[9]

As Worth-Wharton grew, it changed its focus. In 1897, a loan and trust division was added, and in 1900 a banking department was created. In 1903, the company obtained its charter to sell life insurance in North Carolina and, just before making its first sales, officially changed its name to Southern Loan & Trust Company.

Shortly afterward, in 1905, the real estate division of Worth-Wharton spun off to become Southern Real Estate Company, which quickly became one of Greensboro's most successful businesses. Concurrently, Southern Loan & Trust was again renamed, this time calling itself Southern Life & Trust to reflect its growing focus on life insurance. For its logo, Southern Life & Trust chose the locally famous Pilot Mountain, an imposing mass of granite that could be seen from 70 miles away on a clear day. The choice of Pilot Mountain sent a clear message: Southern Life & Trust was "rock ribbed" and firmly planted in local soil.

Management of the company was tight-knit, with responsibilities divided among a group of kin or close friends. E. P. Wharton, a signatory of Worth-Wharton, was the first president of Southern Loan & Trust. Day-to-day management, meanwhile, was entrusted to John Worth's grandson, 41-year-old Alexander Worth "A. W." McAlister. Like Wharton's,

Left: The first claim paid by Southern Loan & Trust in 1904 was on the life of William T. Ellis, who was killed in a railroad accident. The claim was for $1,000.

Opposite: A sample bond issued by Southern Life & Trust. Like most insurance companies of the day, Southern sold bonds to help capitalize its rapid growth.

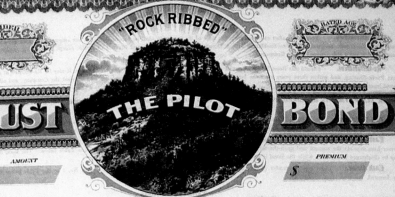

TRUST "ROCK RIBBED" THE PILOT BOND

AMOUNT $ _____   PREMIUM $ _____

Southern Life and Trust Co.

Upon receipt and approval, at its Home Office, of proofs of the death of

_____ the Insured,

of _____ County of _____ State of _____

during the Term ending the _____ day of _____ Nineteen Hundred and _____

or subsequently, if this Bond shall be renewed and continued in force, according to its terms, the

Southern Life and Trust Company

will pay _____ Dollars

Subject to the provisions within stated

to _____ of the Insured.

CHANGE OF BENEFICIARY

Subject to the interest of any assignee, the Insured may change, and successively change, the Beneficiary or Beneficiaries, by notice to the Company, at its Home Office, in writing, accompanied by this Bond, such change to become effective only when endorsed hereon by the Company. If there is no Beneficiary living at the death of the Insured, the amount then insured by this Bond, shall be paid to the Executors, Administrators, or Assigns of the Insured.

THIS BOND SHARES IN THE PROFITS OF THE COMPANY AS HEREIN PROVIDED

At the end of the first Profit-Accumulating Period of this Bond, if the Insured is then living and the premiums have been duly paid hereon until that time, and not otherwise, the Company will apportion to this Bond its distributive share of the Profits, as determined by the Company's Actuary, that have accrued from Profit-Sharing Bonds, and the Insured shall then have a choice of one of the following

METHODS OF SETTLEMENT

1. Withdraw the Profits, in cash, and continue this Bond paid-up for its face amount, for the term stated in Option No. 1, of the Table on next page, sharing in profits; or
2. Convert the Profits into an Annual Income for Life, and continue this Bond paid-up for its face amount, for the term stated in Option No. 1, sharing in profits; or
3. Convert the Full Cash Value, as stated, or the Profits alone, into paid-up insurance, for the term stated in Option No. 1, or for such other term as may be mutually agreed upon and covered by a Policy, sharing in profits (evidence of insurability satisfactory to the Company will be required, for any amount in excess of the face amount of this Bond, and for the whole amount when a part or the whole of the Cash Value of an Endowment Bond is sought to be converted into paid-up Life Insurance); or
4. Convert the Full Cash Value, as stated, into an Annual Income for Life, and surrender this Bond; or
5. Withdraw the Full Cash Value, as stated, in cash, and surrender this Bond.

If this Bond is continued beyond the first Profit-Accumulating Period, profits shall be apportioned at the end of every fifth year thereafter during the continuance of the Bond, under the above provisions.

Not less than thirty days before the end of the first Profit-Accumulating Period, the Company will furnish the Insured a statement in writing showing the results of the Bond under each of the above Methods of Settlement. If within thirty days after the end of the said period the Insured shall have made no selection of a Method of Settlement, the profits will be converted into an Annual Income for Life, and this Bond continued as stated in the second Method.

The First Profit-Accumulating Period of this Bond will end on the _____ Anniversary of the date above written, when its Full Cash Value shall be not less than

_____ Dollars,

and in addition thereto, its then-apportioned share of profits.

MORTUARY DIVIDEND

In the event of the death of the Insured during the First Profit-Accumulating Period, this Bond being then in full force, there will be paid, together with the principal sum insured, a sum equal to twenty per cent. of the total premiums paid hereon, reckoned at the tabular annual rate.

O. L. M. D.

McAlister's roots ran deep with Southern Loan & Trust. In 1895, he had founded one of the "original four" fire insurance companies in Greensboro, the Southern Stock Mutual Insurance Company, which later became the Southern Stock Fire Insurance Company.

A. W. McAlister

A. W. McAlister would have a lasting influence on Southern Life & Trust. Born in March 1862 in Asheboro, North Carolina, he was the son of Alexander Carey and Adelaide Worth McAlister. In 1862 he earned a bachelor of arts degree from the University of North Carolina, then taught school for a short time before becoming an insurance agent in Greensboro.

When E. P. Wharton retired in July 1907, McAlister became president and immediately asserted his influence over Southern Life & Trust. Succeeding in business, he reasoned, would be possible only by paying careful attention to basic fundamentals and by always striving to do the right thing. As the business practices of American corporations began to wield broader influence over citizens, McAlister formed a corporate philosophy based on the Golden Rule and postulated that a corporation could have a heart.

"That 'corporations have no souls' is an ancient maxim of the law and is responsible for several centuries of corporate injustice and inhumanity," he wrote in the inaugural edition of The Pilot newsletter, January 1913.[10]

The idea of a soulless corporation, he continued, was created by lawyers to imply that corporations were not people and could not be jailed as such. But this idea, he felt, had established a double standard that allowed the corporate entity to behave in a way that was immoral.

"Corporations have gotten the habit of living up to the soulless part," he wrote. "Man incorporated has persisted in the perpetuation of arbitrary, dishonest and inhuman policies which the man individual would be ashamed to countenance."[11]

As he continued his indictment, McAlister implored the employees at Southern Life to recognize the essential humanity of their company.

"A corporation does have a soul, a composite soul as the men who constitute and manage it

MCALISTER'S BUSINESS PRINCIPLES

- Make haste slowly.
- Mere bigness does not count.
- Do the right thing and let the consequences take care of themselves.
- Be not too quick to think the other fellow wrong.
- Always take the benefit of the doubt in the selection of men, in the selection of risks, and in the selection of a course of action.
- The only customer worth having is a satisfied customer.
- Let the rule of business be the Golden Rule.

have," he wrote. "There is no such thing as corporate irresponsibility; a corporation cannot trespass against human rights without some individual or individuals being amenable for it. This is the new corporate conscience."[12]

In closing, he made an impassioned plea: "Let us, while we live, endeavor to breathe a spirit into this corporate entity to which we have attached ourselves and labor together to the end, that as it becomes greater it may never grow into a heartless, soulless machine, but that it may have the ineffaceable stamp of individuality and character."[13]

This attitude was reflected in the company's stance toward its employees. McAlister was a well-known health advocate who urged his employees to avoid unhealthy foods and alcohol.[14] The workday also included five minutes for an exercise period, often led by McAlister himself. At the same time every morning, every one in the home office (men and women in separate groups) stood and performed five minutes of calisthenics. On rainy days, an open fire was maintained in the president's

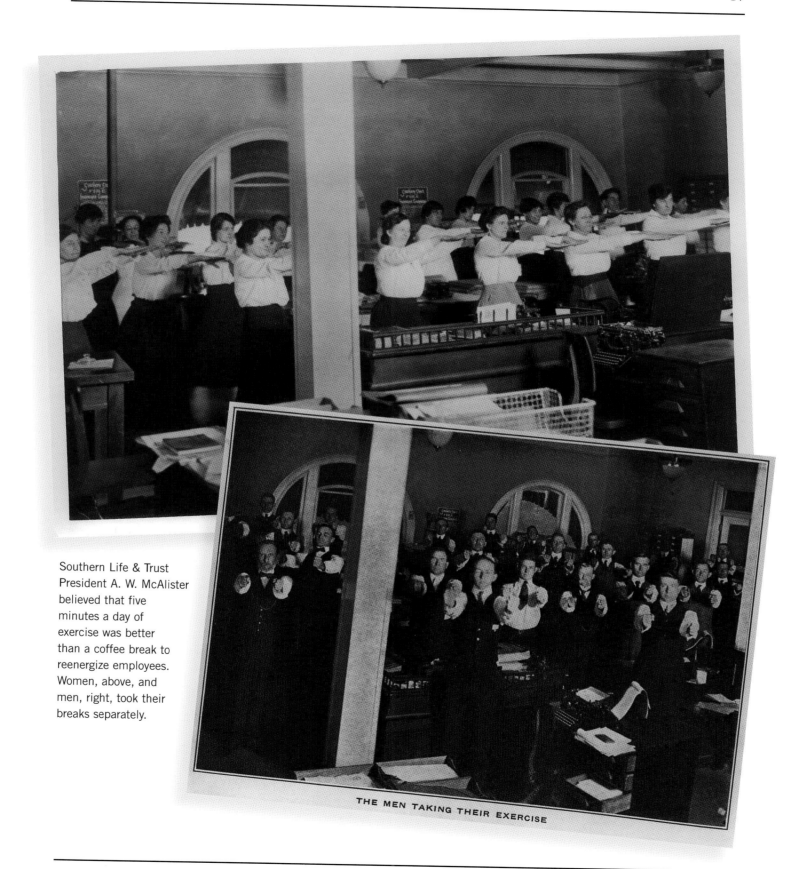

Southern Life & Trust President A. W. McAlister believed that five minutes a day of exercise was better than a coffee break to reenergize employees. Women, above, and men, right, took their breaks separately.

THE MEN TAKING THEIR EXERCISE

Southern Loan & Trust offered a lower premium to anyone who signed an "abstainer's agreement" swearing off drugs and alcohol. Tobacco, however, was permitted.

office for employees to dry off before heading to their work stations.

When it came to expanding the company, McAlister did not view high principles and aggressive management as mutually exclusive. Successful, growing companies employed people and created wealth, and McAlister saw this as part of the social contract. Toward that end, he announced that Southern Life & Trust would not immediately pay dividends to shareholders, who were mostly officers of the company. Instead, profits were plowed back into basic business-building activities like establishing a client list and creating a strong balance sheet.

McAlister was also a shrewd marketer, tapping into southern pride and resentment against northern insurance companies. In a letter soliciting business, he wrote, "For one hundred years the North has been growing richer and richer because we have persisted in buying insurance and other things there instead of producing them here."[15]

McAlister was also a tough actuary, giving discounted rates to those who signed "abstainer" agreements vowing off alcohol and drug use outside of religious ceremonies or cooking. Tobacco use, however, was permitted under the agreement, which covered only "vinous, spirituous or malt liquors; opium, morphine, laudanum, chloral, cocaine or other narcotic."

His risk-minimizing tactics worked splendidly. During the first three years of the company's life insurance operations, the mortality record for 1,600 policy holders totaled two deaths, one from appendicitis and one from a railroad wreck. With more than $2 million worth of insurance in force, it was an enviable record, and dividends were finally

A. W. McAlister in his office at Southern Life & Trust. McAlister was a firm moralist who believed that corporations had an obligation to their communities, and that in turn, employees had an obligation to their corporations.

declared in May 1907, with payouts ranging from 15 percent to 20 percent.

By 1913, the company had more than $2 million worth of insurance in force, and better than 10 percent of paid-for business came from existing policy holders.

Southern Life Leads the Way

McAlister saw the corporation as a sum of its people, and he set a high standard for personal conduct in the community. For more than three decades, McAlister himself was deeply involved in his state. He was active in the North Carolina Conference for Social Service from its formation in 1912 and served as its president from 1915 to 1916. He also served as vice chairman of the North Carolina State Board of Charities and Public Welfare

PROGRAMME

Hundred Thousand Dollar Club

of the

SOUTHERN LIFE AND TRUST CO.

GREENSBORO, NORTH CAROLINA

$100,000.00

August 19, 20, 21, 1914

Grove Park Inn

SUNSET MOUNTAIN, ... ASHEVILLE, N. C.

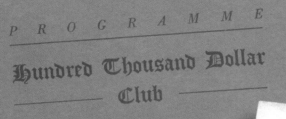

Opposite: Southern Life adopted Pilot Mountain as its logo, sponsoring trips and outings to the famous site. On a fair day, Pilot Mountain could be seen from 70 miles away.

Right: A Southern Life employee plays golf, a game that was unknown in the South until McAlister imported the state's first set of clubs from Canada and opened the first public golf course.

Below: In addition to his leadership role at Southern Life, McAlister also organized a number of other insurance companies, including Pilot Fire Insurance Company and McAlister, Vaughn & Scales, an investment and real estate company.

in 1917 and remained on the board until 1944. Closer to home, he served as president of the Greensboro Board of Public Welfare and president of the Greensboro Council of Catholics, Jews, and Protestants.[16]

Golf was a game unknown to Southerners when McAlister brought home five sets of clubs from a Canadian fishing trip in 1908. Opening a free, five-hole pitch-and-putt course on the northwest corner of Summit Avenue and Dewey Street, he became the father of golf in Guilford County. Two years later he built a $500 clubhouse, complete with lockers, and in 1911 the prestigious Greensboro Country Club opened on the site.

As the company grew, it began to create traditions that would last for decades. The first recorded employee retreat and conference was held August

PILOT FIRE INSURANCE COMPANY
A SOUTHERN COMPANY

THE PILOT

McALISTER, VAUGHN & SCALES INC.
GENERAL AGENTS
GREENSBORO, N. C.

19–21, 1914, at the four-star Grove Park Inn in Asheville, North Carolina. In 1916, Southern Life began reserving a train and taking its entire staff to Pilot Mountain for a day trip. The company sponsored its first golf tournament in 1919, an annual highlight that continued for more than 70 years.

Southern Life was growing quickly in revenue and stature, but these were nevertheless hard times for many people. In the early 1900s, the company newsletter promoted overall health, steering people away from whiskey and cautioning that germs were spread by houseflies, well water, and casual human contact. Disease nevertheless took its toll. In 1913, an outbreak of typhoid fever cost Southern Life $2,500 in life insurance claims, and tuberculosis claimed the lives of three Southern Life employees.

In response, Southern Life opened the Health and Conservation Department—one of the nation's first health insurance services. A company physician went door-to-door among policy holders and offered free physical exams. The hope was to diagnose untreated disease and offer preventive help, allowing policy holders to "get entirely well and prolong life several and often many years."

There were considerable misgivings about the plan at first, and many company officials were doubtful as to how it would be received. But policy holders "presented themselves in great numbers to be examined, and with an unexpected degree of enthusiasm."[17]

By 1914, with World War I just beginning in Europe, Southern Life & Trust had $3,576,500 in paid-for insurance. A year later, with the United States warily avoiding the war, McAlister announced an ambitious goal: Southern Life would achieve $5 million worth of insurance in force by 1916. With $4.05 million in force in 1915—the highest ever—this seemed entirely possible.[18] To get there, Southern Life continued its innovative marketing techniques. In 1916 the company introduced a savings plan that enabled low-income individuals to afford a life insurance policy and the wealthy to afford more insurance.

A year later, Southern Life & Trust became one of three corporate sponsors of North Carolina's Moving Picture Health Car. Motion pictures were a new phenomenon in 1917, and the board of health began sending around a car outfitted with a Victrola motion picture machine and camping gear for its driver, technician, and lecturer. The Moving Picture Health Car visited counties across the state and gave open-air showings of health education films. After watching short films on dental care, care and feeding of babies, and illnesses including malaria, typhoid fever, and tuberculosis, anyone who asked for more information received literature provided by Southern Life & Trust, Metropolitan Life Insurance Company, and the Colgate Company.

War Times

These good years took place against an increasingly dismal backdrop of war and unrest. Overseas, World War I had bogged down along a line of soggy trenches through western Europe. Sickness, machines guns, and poison gas inflicted casualties by the thousands, with neither party gaining advantage. America, under President Woodrow Wilson, worked strenuously to avoid the war—a task that became increasingly complicated as Britain appealed for help and German U-boats stalked American merchant shipping in the Atlantic. By 1916, it appeared less a question of "if" America would enter the war than of "when."

Insurance companies played an important part in America's shift to war footing. As the cost of supplying Britain and developing an army soared, the government turned to Liberty Bonds, which were sold by insurance companies. "Men!" began a popular poster signed by Uncle Sam, "Every American who considers himself a man, and is able, and not otherwise serving me, will buy a Liberty Bond. Further explanations are unnecessary."

In 1917, after the sinking of the *Lusitania*, America finally joined the war, shipping hundreds of thousands of troops across the Atlantic to the muddy trenches in Europe. American intervention would tip the scales in favor of the Allies, and it would have an immediate effect on the life insurance industry.

In the first two months of 1917, as the fear of war mounted, Southern Life sold almost as much life insurance as it had in the first five months of 1916. In all, insurance in force increased 284 percent between 1910 and 1916, while assets increased 326 percent. Dividends paid to policy holders in 1916 totaled $53,233, while death claim payments were $57,782. A year later, Southern Life broke the $5 million goal, ending the year with $6.6 million worth of insurance in force.

This success would come at great cost, however. While insurance in force rose quickly, so did death claims as widows of soldiers killed in action turned to their greatest source of financial stability. Worse yet, this tragedy was exacerbated by a domestic tragedy. Between 1914 and 1918, a global flu epidemic killed approximately 20 million people, including hundreds of thousands of Americans. This toll had a dampening effect on economic activity in America, and it too increased death claims.

In the years leading up to 1920, while insurance in force was rising quickly, many insurance companies announced reduced dividends. Even after the war ended, Southern Life & Trust continued to see increased business, partly because of this flu epidemic. Like other companies, however, its dividends were also placed in jeopardy. By 1919, the company had $16 million in delivered business, an increase of nearly 100 percent over the previous year.

The rapid expansion strained Southern Life's resources because the first year's premium was not

Opposite: Southern Life & Trust broke new ground when it began sending physicians to make house calls on policy holders. The idea was to offer preventative medicine for greater health.

PART 4

CONFIDENTIAL REPORT OF MEDICAL EXAMINER.

[After answering Question 15, dismiss the applicant unless a woman, and rely on your own knowledge or information.]

1. A. How long have you known (Full Name) _William Thomas Allis_ the party examined? _10 yrs, #15_

   B. Party's occupation (if more than one, state all): _Rural mail carrier_

   C. State exact nature of duties required _Over mail routes on line & collecting & delivering & annual_
   all miles

2. Give an accurate description of the party in the following particulars: (Be accurate as to weight and height.)

Race	Caucasian	Girth of Chest, under the Vest		Form of Chest	Figure		Eyes	Blue	Condition of Skin		Physical Defects or Deformities

| Nationality | American | 41 inches | round | stout | | Hair | Dark | smooth | | none | |

| Weight | Height | Girth of Waist | Forced Respiration | Forced Inspiration | General Appearance (Healthy or Unhealthy) | | Complexion | fair | Bones: Large or Small | large | Does Applicant appear Older than age given? no |

| 218 lbs. | 5ft 6in. | 42 in. | 43 in | 38 in | healthy | | fair | | | | What is the Apparent Age? 33 |

3. Are the weight, height and girth measurements reasonably proportionate? (Consult table.) _Yes_
   If not, state whether either parent or other of their children exhibit a like peculiarity,

4. A. Give particulars of any INJURY or ILLNESS during the past ten years _Typhoid fever_   B. Dates _88_
   C. Duration _5 weeks_   D. Sequelæ

5. A. Are the **Respiratory Murmur** and Percussion Note clear, distinct, and of normal character over all parts of both LUNGS?   A. _Yes_
   B. Is the **Respiration** full, easy and regular?   B. _Yes_
   C. Does the physical examination reveal anything whatever abnormal in the condition of the **RESPIRATORY ORGANS**?   C. _No_

6. A. Is there any ...
   B. Give the ...
   C. Does it ...
      If the pa ...
   D. Did you ...

7. What is the ...

8. Urinary Ana ...   Albumin _none_   Sugar _none_

9. How do you ...

10. Are the Fun ...

11. Has the par ...   ...ency to disease? _no_

12. Do you disc ... ment, p ...   ...stitutional Disease? _no_

13. Has he the s ...

14. Has the party ...

15. Has the party ...and follow an attack of that affection
    manifest u ...and physically, as before the attack? _no_

16. Do you find a ... History, Re ... or danger? ...

17. Does he speci ...

18. Is there any i ... been such as ...   ...ther than a MORAL and TEMPERATE life, or that his habits are or have

19. Do his manner ...

20. From the infor ... health and s ...   ...on in your possession that is reliable, do you consider the party in perfect

21. Do you conside ...

22. Do you recomm ...

23.

A. Is she pregnant ...   **APPLICANT IS A WOMAN.**
B. Is her menstrual ...   ...dren has she had? _____ The age of the last
C. Has she passed ...   ...dence of uterine disease? _____
D. Has she ever ...   ...band's occupation? _____
                             ...t marriage? _____

Remarks.—Here ...

I CERTIFY ...

Examined at ...

this _27_ day ...

...the foregoing answers are in my own handwriting.

_M. D._

Medical Examiner for the Company.

"ROCK RIBBED"

THE PILOT

Twenty-One Points

WHEREIN

The Southern Life and Trust Co.

IS UNIQUE

◻ ◻ ◻

ORGANIZATION	-	**SEVEN POINTS**
METHODS	- -	**SEVEN POINTS**
RESULTS	- -	**SEVEN POINTS**

Jefferson Standard and Southern Life created ads that educated consumers about the benefits of life insurance, including financial protection and security for families.

"Papa, Are We Protected"

We are the people, and our wants should be provided for, give us good homes, plenty to eat, comfortable clothes, give us education, training and pure society, give us protection in a good life insurance company for we are entitled to the best and should have it. We are to inherit the earth. Prepare us for this great responsibility by giving us what we demand and we will become honest, industrious, upright citizens, proud of our ancestry and loyal to our country.

Copyright 1911, Amer. Litho. & Ptg. Co., Des Moines

The Wail of Your Family

Closed on Your Home?

WANTED—By a widow lady with two small children a situation as housekeeper. Widower preferred. Add. Mrs. J., Herald.

WANTED—A situation by a young lady as copyist. Has a family to support. Address Mary L., Examiner Office.

WANTED—A boy twelve years of age desires a place where he can earn something to aid in support of a family. Address Mrs. W., Chronicle Office.

WANTED—A home for three orphan children of good parentage. Address City Mission. Phone x 37.

WANTED—By a young lady, daughter of formerly wealthy parents, position in refined home to perform any duties. Home wanted. Urgent reply, Box 224, Bee.

Will the Mortgage be

Imagine, if you please, your widow asking for a position that she may support the children for whom you were responsible. Think of your little boy seeking employment that he may aid, *at the expense of his education*, in the support of your family. Picture your daughter asking for work that she may provide the necessities of life for herself and others dear to you. *All this because you neglected to secure*

This is Life Insurance

for them the comforts which life insurance money will give.

It's dangerous. The gamble on death amounts to billions of dollars staked on the beat of the human heart. The races are ever on, while Life and Death are ceaseless rivals, pitted against each other for the rich prizes offered by that marvelous institution, Life Insurance.

Rev. Dr. Talmage has well said: "If there be anything more pitiable than a woman delicately brought up, and on her marriage day given by an indulgent father to a man to whom she is the chief joy and pride of life until the moment of his death, and then that same woman going out with helpless children at her back to struggle for bread in a world where brawny muscle and rugged souls are necessary—I say, if there is anything more pitiable than that I do not know what it is."

"Some one has said, 'I believe when I go

rd will provide for the poorhouses of show you, how God ed children of ne- is, He provides for arity. As for my- e the Lord provide ate home, through arental affection." r length, Mr. Mar-

l lay a lily on your indly tribute upon you away and pro- en you go will the house? When you will your orphans The best time to

mselves wings and fly away, but life insurance, suspended on the brittle thread of human life like a benison above the heads of the helpless, suddenly loosed by the snapping asunder of the silver cord, drops into the lap of the widow. Such is life insurance, *if you have it.*

SEE IMMEDIATELY AN AGENT OF THE

JEFFERSON STANDARD LIFE
INSURANCE COMPANY
GREENSBORO, - NORTH CAROLINA

Over $118,000,000.00 insurance in force.

Surplus to protect policyholders over $1,300,000.00.

Paid to policyholders since organization and now held for their benefit, over $15,000,000.00.

enough to pay the acquisition expenses (agent's commission, examiner's fee, inspection report cost, state and federal taxes, and other expenses). Explaining to shareholders that upcoming dividends might be lower than expected, McAlister wrote, "The fact that the company is able to pay dividends at all in 1920 is a source of gratification."[19]

He ended 1919 by imploring agents to preach the gospel of thrift: "There is no better motto for 1920 than Work and Save."[20]

A Friendly Neighbor

When Southern Life & Trust closed the books on its 17th year of business, it operated in a much different environment from the one in which it had been founded in 1903. When Southern Life was created, the Wright brothers had just taken humanity's first flight, automobile registrations still numbered in the hundreds, the telephone was but a distant dream, and America had just begun to project its military might overseas.

Southern Life was among the first purely southern financial institutions to rise up in a region that was just developing its own financial and industrial identity. Ultimately, however, there was room enough in North Carolina for more than one locally grown life insurance company. In 1907, four years after Southern Life & Trust (then Southern Loan & Trust) sold its first policy, Jefferson Standard Life Insurance Company was organized in Raleigh, North Carolina. The relationship between Southern Life & Trust and Jefferson Standard, close neighbors and friendly competitors, would define the life insurance industry in North Carolina into the next century.

Jefferson Standard was established in 1906 by brothers P. D. and Charles Gold. The Gold brothers sought to build a successful southern institution that would turn a profit while leading the South out of a farming economy. Like the founders of Southern Life & Trust, they observed that southern money was too often flowing northward to financial institutions that weren't always focused on the regional market. As *The State* magazine explained, "The time had come to shake off the domination of far-removed financial interests in order that the South might regain its rightful place politically and financially."[21]

The Gold brothers were perfectly suited to start a large financial services company. They were financially sophisticated, having grown up in a newspaper family in Wilson, North Carolina. They envisioned a company that would operate with uncompromising ethics, one that could withstand financial shocks and enrich North Carolina. Its core product would be permanent, cash-value life insurance.

Originally, they sought to raise $500,000 to create Jefferson Standard Life Insurance Company, but selling stock for a complicated financial company was an uphill battle in the rural, pine-forested state, where horses were just beginning to be replaced by rail cars. To make matters more difficult, in the midst of their stock offering in 1907, the United States suffered a panic as a number of banks failed and cash payments were suspended throughout the country.

As a result, cash was almost totally unavailable, loans were curtailed, and the sale of stock became practically impossible, all of which eventually led Congress to pass the Federal Reserve System Act, providing an elastic currency—a cash supply that would match public demand. The 1913 act didn't come in time to help the Gold brothers in their drive to create Jefferson Standard. Finally, P. D. Gold hatched a plan he promptly sold to the state's insurance commissioner and several banks in the area.

It was the state's most unusual stock offering, patterned after the arrangement that was helping New York's banks get back on their feet. Several national banks operating in North Carolina agreed to loan selected subscribers a percentage of the face value of the company stock, with the shares as collateral. The proceeds were deposited to the credit of Jefferson Standard.

"Thus my brother and I were able to place the remaining shares for over $350,000 within sixty days," P. D. Gold explained later.[22]

Two dozen individuals stepped forward to buy stock in the new company, and on May 27, 1907, the first organizational meeting was held. The original shareholders included George A. Holderness, of Tarboro, North Carolina, whose son, Howard "Chick" Holderness, would later become president. Another prominent founder was Albert G. Myers Sr., of Gastonia, North Carolina, already eminent in banking and textiles. Myers served as a board director of Jefferson Standard from 1911 until his retirement in 1970. George A. Grimsley was another of the key organizers.

Ultimately, the company boasted capital stock of $250,000, with an equal amount in paid-in surplus, and 298 shareholders. On August 8, 1907, newspapers statewide carried the story that North Carolina's largest corporation had been created. In the state capital, the *Metro Daily* called it the largest initial capitalization of a North Carolina corporation. Its own publisher, Josephus Daniels, was an initial stockholder. Later a *Greensboro Daily News* article looking back on the company's founding declared that "from that [first] date the company went sailing like a strong clipper ship with a steady wind over her stern quarter."[23]

The first policy sold by Jefferson Standard Life, in the amount of $5,000, was bought by company president Joseph G. Brown. The new company boasted the largest initial capitalization of a North Carolina corporation.

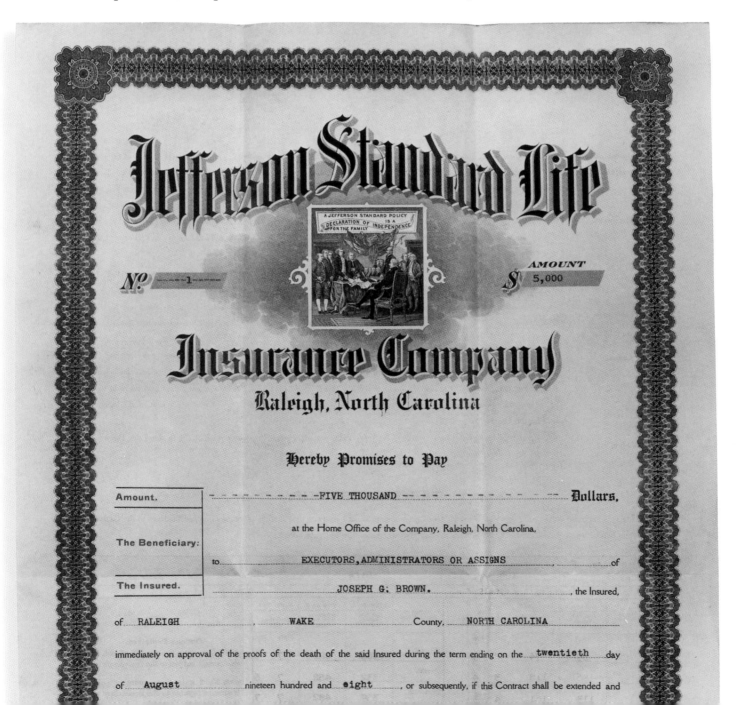

PLEASANT DANIEL GOLD

BORN IN 1876, PLEASANT DANIEL GOLD was a native of Wilson, North Carolina, and obtained a degree in 1898 from the University of North Carolina. He studied law at Richmond College and attended the Pulitzer School of Journalism at Columbia University in New York before founding Jefferson Standard Life Insurance Company in 1907 with his brother, Charles. The other Gold brother, John D. Gold, became editor of the *Wilson Daily Times.*

At their first meeting on August 15, 1912, the company agents presented P. D. Gold with a finely polished ebony cane as he stepped down from the helm of Jefferson Standard. Its elaborately engraved gold head declared it was "A Token of Esteem" from the agency association of Jefferson Standard.

The articulate, civic-minded Gold was an industry leader, serving on the executive committee of the American Life Convention and as its president in 1911. He was a founding board member of the state orphanage, the Children's Home Society of North Carolina.

After leaving the company, he moved to California and became involved in movie production. A shrewd fundraiser, he went on to found the National Drama Corporation in New York City and remained in the motion picture business until 1920. A few years later,

the National Drama studio was sold to the Fox Film Company.

A historian, Gold moved to Florida and became the state's official chronicler during the 1920s. He served as mayor of Daytona Beach (then called Seabreeze) and wrote four historical books on the area, many of which were still in use in local schools in the 1970s. Gold wrote a family history, *Gold Generations in England and America,* that became the prototype for amateur geneaology.

A federal appointment in 1934 to the Board of Veterans Appeals took him to Washington, and in 1943 he was appointed to the War Bond committee.[1]

At the age of 73, Gold signed up as a Jefferson Standard agent in Silver Spring, Maryland. Eight years later he passed the baton officially, presenting his gold-crowned cane to Karl Ljung, senior vice president of agency operations.

Gold continued with the company, servicing corporate pension plans until he retired in 1961.[2] He died in Maryland on March 2, 1965, after living in a nursing home for several years.

P. D. Gold's simple road to happiness, which he put into poetic form and often quoted, was, "Something to do you like to do / someone to love who loves you, too / something to hope for along life's path / abiding faith in the aftermath."

The Jefferson Standard logo depicts Jefferson signing the Declaration of Independence. From its first days, Jefferson Standard grew extremely fast.

holders' notes were liquidated, the bonds repurchased by the banks, and the collateral loan paid."[24]

Freedom for the Family

Besides uncompromising ethics, P. D. Gold and his brother Charles had a definite vision for their company. P. D. Gold once wrote that his policy holders were the "great middle class of American citizenship, the backbone of the company." This spirit led company leaders to select Thomas Jefferson as a namesake. At the time, Jefferson, the third president of the United States, represented moral conduct yet was accessible to regular people and championed the rights of the individual.

When Jefferson Standard sought to create a logo, it turned once again to the patriotic imagery of its namesake. The first Jefferson Standard logo was inspired by a John Trumbull painting of the signers of the Declaration of Independence. P. D. Gold found an etching of the original, pasted the company's slogan at the top, and the company's new logo was born. The company slogan emerged as "A Jefferson Standard policy is a declaration of independence for the family."

A Move to Greensboro

By the end of 1907, Jefferson Standard had already issued more than $1 million in insurance, all of it in North Carolina. This achievement, which took less than half a year, was all the more impressive because of the troubles in the banking industry. Several banks closed their doors that year, including the Knickerbockers Trust Company, and others suspended operations indefinitely. To reassure a skeptical public, Congress created the Federal Reserve System to shore up the shaky banking industry.

Spurred onward by its early success, Jefferson Standard looked to quickly expand its reach. In 1909, the company crossed the state line and began selling life insurance in South Carolina. By the end of that year, the two-year-old company had $9 million of insurance in force, leading the company to adopt the advertising slogan "Giant of the South."[25] Within two years, Jefferson agents were selling insurance in Georgia and Alabama.

As it spread, Jefferson Standard was already becoming known for its edgy advertising. One brazen

There were only 111 insurance companies in the nation the day Jefferson Standard Life Insurance Company opened for business. The first policy was written August 7, 1907, to Joseph Gill Brown, the new company president. Brown, who would hold the post for five years, was also president of Citizens National Bank in Raleigh and was considered one of the South's leading bankers. Company founder P. D. Gold was elected first vice president and general manager. The secretary was H. G. Chatfield, of Greensboro, and the treasurer was J. Parker, of Raleigh.

Jefferson Standard got off to an exceedingly good start. Within six months, almost $1 million in insurance had been written, and the company was ready to address the bonds taken out by its original shareholders to finance its creation. Ownership of the bonds was transferred to Jefferson Standard, paid for out of bank credits created by the sale of insurance company stock. Thus, wrote P. D. Gold, "The plan worked successfully, eventually the share-

A Jefferson Standard brochure pointed out the local benefits of buying insurance from a North Carolina company. At the time, most insurance was sold by companies headquartered in northern states.

THE STORY OF TWO DOLLARS

EACH SPENT IN THE SOUTH BUT—

THE JEFFERSON STANDARD
LIFE INSURANCE COMPANY

GREENSBORO   NORTH CAROLINA

HARRISON PRINTING CO., GREENSBORO, N. C.

ON JANUARY 1, 1917, Two Dollars were spent by different men but both in a city in that part of the United States usually designated as "The South." The story of these two dollars during the past year will be of interest to the man who wishes to do the best for himself and his Southland. Each dollar was spent for insurance. One was part of $35 which was paid for a policy in the Mammoth Life Insurance Company of New York. The other was part of $35 which was spent for a life insurance policy in the Jefferson Standard Life Insurance Co., Greensboro, N. C.

The first went through the usual banking channels to New York and there was held in a vault of the Mammoth Life Insurance Company of New York for about three months, and then, with thousands of other dollars was used to purchase the bonds of a large factory in Massachusetts. This dollar, with others, contributed in its way to the employment of many men in a New England enterprise, and helped to build up an industry which is competing with Southern industries. After having been spent for the bonds of this mill, it was turned loose in the thriving mill town of_____, in New England, paid many debts, and contributed, as every dollar does, to the material welfare and prosperity of everything with which it came in contact. As it rolled along in its merry way, doing good to the New Englanders, it jingled jauntily with many other dollars which had come from the Southland, and which, as it touched its bright neighbors seemed to wonder, "Why am I so far away from home; why could I not remain in the Southland and do this same good there? Are there so many dollars in that country that they want to get rid of them, and am I not needed there as much as I am here?"

The story of the other dollar, the one which was spent for a life insurance policy in the JEFFERSON, of Greensboro, is just as interesting.

It was paid into a local bank. Within three weeks it was loaned, with many other dollars, to a Southern man, who, having confidence in his section was developing his farm and needed this money to build better barns, a better home, and improve his land. This particular dollar was paid by this man to a carpenter who was at work on his barn. By the carpenter it was paid to his doctor. It was used by the doctor to pay the doctor's monthly grocery bill. The grocer used it, with other dollars, to pay his druggist's bill. The druggist used it to pay his neighbor for some vegetables. From there it went to the local butcher. From him it went through many other hands, and eventually paid hundreds of dollars of debts. As it jingled along on its merry course, doing good in every case, its little song was, "Just see how much good I can do in the Southland, where I am so badly needed, and where I can do my greatest good because I am needed."

Eventually, with nine hundred and ninety-nine more dollars, it went to a poor widow whose husband had just died, and the Thousand Dollar policy which she held in the JEFFERSON, contributed to a very large extent to alleviate her unhappy condition by enabling her to care for her little ones and to educate them.

Moral.—Why will Southern people continue to send their money to the North for life insurance, when they have in the South a Company that is not only the strongest regular Life Insurance Company in the South, but offers ideal policy contracts as cheap as is consistent with safe insurance.

poster showed a cow drawn over a map of the United States. The cow was being fed in the South and milked in the Northeast. The caption read: "Why send your life insurance premiums to New York, Massachusetts, Connecticut and other northeastern cities when they could be kept at home and invested locally?"

Like other insurance salespeople, Jefferson Standard salesmen had to explain how insurance worked. According to a Jefferson Standard sales training manual from the early 1900s, insurance was "a method of distributing an individual's loss among a large number of other persons who are willing to assume each his small share of it, in return for the certainty that if a similar loss falls upon any one of them, the loser, or those dependent upon him, will in like manner be indemnified."[26]

Although Jefferson Standard was growing quickly, it ran into other difficulties that were common to all insurance companies. Like Southern Life, Jefferson Standard officers sought to put profits back into the business rather than pay out dividends. Board minutes from 1910 observed, "The future is fraught with difficulties. The way to profit is long, the task is arduous, and the cost is great."[27]

Naturally, however, the company's shareholders were anxious to see a return on their investment. They pointed to other insurance companies in the state, few of which could boast Jefferson Standard's rapid growth but were still paying dividends. The directors stuck with their policy, and in 1912 they declined once again to issue a dividend. They argued there was not yet enough insurance in force to make a profit. Incensed shareholders pointed out that some of them had bought their stock on credit and were paying interest on the loan without receiving any dividend to offset the expense. When no dividends were forthcoming, shareholders began to sell off their stock, driving the price of Jefferson Standard capital stock from $100 per share to $55 per share.

Opposite: Policies from the Greensboro Life Insurance Company and Security Life and Annuity. Although relatively small, Greensboro was a hotbed of insurance companies because of the efforts of a few dedicated organizers and company founders, including the founders of both Jefferson Standard and Southern Life.

The falling value of the company led P. D. Gold to write, "It was evident to all that increase of insurance in force and reduction of expenses by consolidation or merger with other companies was the only solution."

He turned to a close friend, Julian Price, who was secretary of the Greensboro Life Insurance Company and would later be credited with the company's "Giant of the South" slogan and the cow poster. The two began discussing a merger between Jefferson Standard and Greensboro Life Insurance Company. The merger would be an exchange of stock, with no cash involved.

Because secrecy was important, 12 men were appointed from the directors of each company. To avoid publicity, the 24 men met in the Metropolitan Hotel in Washington, D.C. During the discussion, it was clear that the merger would go forward. Instead, the directors focused on the name of the new company and its location. Jefferson Standard was located in Raleigh, whereas Greensboro Life was headquartered in Greensboro.

The exact discussions are lost to history, but P. D. Gold later wrote that the committee was split down the middle over where a new company would be headquartered. Some historians say that P. D. Gold, a former Greensboro resident, wanted the home office located in Greensboro.[28] Others say that Jefferson Standard wanted to remain in Raleigh.

After a split vote, the committee recessed for dinner, came back, and tried again. Again the vote was split. During a midnight recess, several members of the Jefferson board of directors approached Gold, stressed that a failure to merge would damage both companies, and pressed him to break the tie.

He returned to the meeting and proposed a compromise: The new company would be Jefferson Standard Life Insurance Company with home offices in Greensboro. His decision was a practical one, based on a delicate negotiation, but it also made sense for the company. Greensboro was a progressive village set among rolling hills and had boasted daily rail service since 1856.[29]

The directors agreed to the compromise and took the deal back to their shareholders. Before it could be approved, however, a Raleigh-based group of shareholders filed suit to stop the merger and thus the move to Greensboro. Other Raleigh share-

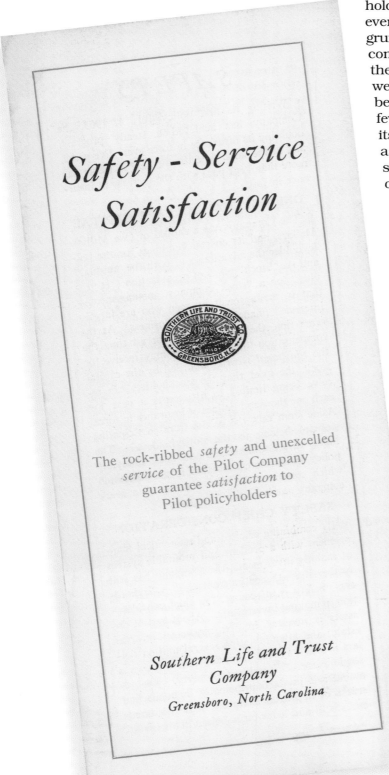

Safety - Service Satisfaction

The rock-ribbed *safety* and unexcelled *service* of the Pilot Company guarantee *satisfaction* to Pilot policyholders

Southern Life and Trust Company
Greensboro, North Carolina

holders began to sell their stock. Ultimately, however, the lawsuit would be resolved, and the disgruntled Raleigh investors simply bowed out of the company while the other shareholders agreed to the merger. In September 1912, while the details were still being worked out, Jefferson Standard began shipping records to Greensboro. Within a few months, Jefferson Standard had completed its relocation. Following the move, most Raleigh associates withdrew, and many of the original shareholders sold their stock, with the exception of the Gold brothers.[30]

New Leadership Emerges

Immediately after the merger, the new company was strapped for capital. Once again, P. D. Gold looked for a merger partner. This time, Jefferson Standard proposed a merger with Security Life and Annuity Company, a Greensboro company that P. D. Gold had helped organize in 1910.

Accounts vary as to who needed whom in the deal. Security was a mutual company without capital requirements and had more insurance in force than the other two. Aubrey Lee Brooks, a Greensboro lawyer and author, later wrote that Jefferson Standard and Greensboro Life Insurance had both written so much business that they had depleted their surpluses and were in dire need of capital.[31]

Whatever the case, the merger was soon approved, and in late 1912, North Carolina newspapers reported the merger of Jefferson Standard with two Greensboro companies, Security Life and Annuity Company and Greensboro Life Insurance Company. Once again, the merger would alter the basic operations of Jefferson Standard. As part of the deal, Security Life and Annuity

Long before it was officially named "The Pilot," Southern Life & Trust was known by that name. This customer satisfaction brochure calls Southern Life "the Pilot Company."

George A. Grimsley was the president of Jefferson Standard from 1912 to 1919. In addition to his work at Jefferson Standard, Grimsley was known for bringing public education to Greensboro.

officers demanded that the new company retain two of its officers in addition to one from Jefferson and one from Greensboro Life. In order to consolidate leadership of the new company, P. D. Gold resigned.

On September 14, the three-way consolidation was completed. The new, much larger Jefferson Standard began operating out of the Fisher building at the northwest corner of Market and Elm Streets. From there, it would grow quickly, occupying space in seven other buildings within a few years. The new company president was George A. Grimsley, a founder of Security Life. Julian Price, from Jefferson Standard, was named vice president. Before the

year was out, capital stock was increased from $250,000 to $350,000 and the company began paying dividends.

When he assumed control over Jefferson Standard, Grimsley was already widely admired in Greensboro as "the father of public schools," having come to the area in 1890 as superintendent. He ran Jefferson Standard until 1919. The following year, he founded Security Life and Trust and in 1924 moved it to nearby Winston-Salem at the urging of the city's business interests. That company would later evolve into Integon Life Insurance Corporation.

When Grimsley stepped down in 1919, Julian Price was named president of Jefferson Standard.[32] By this time, the company had grown dramatically, driven by the same forces that had pushed its crosstown competitor Southern Life & Trust. World War I had just ended, and a virulent flu epidemic was still gaining strength. The flu would claim more lives than the fighting. As happened so often in history, these trying times caused more and more people to turn to life insurance, and insurance companies had ample opportunity to prove their value to the widows and orphans who relied so heavily on their sound investment and financial help.

As the second decade of the twentieth century drew to an end, an anxious country headed into a new world, seemingly beset on all sides. After the 1917 Bolshevik revolution in Russia, Americans were afraid that the United States would fall to communism. The fear reached its height that summer when a street bomb in Manhattan killed more than thirty people and a revolutionary group claimed credit. Finally, soldiers who had gone overseas to war as liberators came home deeply disillusioned. The hopelessness spawned by World War I gave rise to a nihilistic, hollow hedonism best expressed in F. Scott Fitzgerald's novel *The Great Gatsby*.

Yet in their corner of the country, Southern Life & Trust and Jefferson Standard continued to grow quickly, helping thousands of people plan for their futures, strengthening the regional economy, and further developing the relationship that would help carry them through the decades ahead.

The Jefferson Standard building in downtown Greensboro in the 1920s.

CHAPTER TWO

A WORLD OF CHANGE

1920–1939

[It will generate] a generous rivalry, a rivalry between friends, and ought to stimulate us to our very best.

—A. W. McAlister
President, Pilot Life, 1907–1932

A N ANXIOUS COUNTRY HEADED into the 1920s. After a summer of sickness, unrest, and disillusion, still coping with the horrible aftermath of World War I, the United States was swept up in deep-rooted social change. On one hand, the Nineteenth Amendment was passed in 1920, extending suffrage to women. On the other hand, the 1919 Eighteenth Amendment outlawed the consumption of alcohol and ushered in Prohibition. Across the country, hemlines inched up as women experienced new freedom, while speakeasies flowed with jazz and bootleg alcohol. At Southern Life & Trust, A. W. McAlister preached the virtues of abstinence, writing that alcohol and business had no place together.

The tenure of these expansive times was reflected in Jefferson Standard's and Southern Life & Trust's bottom lines. Between 1914 and 1919, both companies grew quickly. With so many insurance companies in town (many of which were founded by the principal Jefferson Standard and Southern Life & Trust), Greensboro earned the nickname "Hartford of the South," a nod to Hartford, Connecticut, and its domination of the insurance industry.

Yet there was a sobering undercurrent. Even as insurance in force grew, the mortality rate of insureds was historically high, often running at more than 100 percent of projections. During the influenza crisis of 1918, 1919, and part of 1920,

Jefferson Standard paid out more than $500,000 for influenza claims alone. Nevertheless, the company managed to pay dividends to shareholders in 1919.[1]

In 1920, the year after Julian Price became president of Jefferson Standard, the company's assets reached $100 million. By year-end, new business had climbed to nearly $50 million, five times the annual rate of the previous five years.

Price's influence on Jefferson Standard would permanently change the company. Indeed, his leadership and personality would reflect not only on Jefferson Standard, but on all of North Carolina. Price was a shrewd marketer who had once sold snuff. He was a formal man who usually wore a white linen suit and carried a gold-tipped cane and fit the mold of a witty and charming southern gentleman.

When it came to building an insurance company, Price's business instincts were above reproach. As early as 1920, he recognized that expansion would be the key to Jefferson Standard's future, and he pushed the company to grow aggressively. In February 1920, just after his appointment,

Pilot Life maintained a high profile in the community through its various printed materials. This calendar promoted Pilot Life in the 1920s.

he targeted 24 new regions for Jefferson Standard: Oklahoma, Missouri, Kansas, Indiana, Ohio, Michigan, Illinois, New Jersey, Delaware, Nebraska, North Dakota, South Dakota, Iowa, Pennsylvania, Cuba, Canal Zone, Puerto Rico, Arizona, New Mexico, Colorado, Utah, Wyoming, Montana, and Idaho. Not all of these territories were reached right away, but operations extended into a total of 14 states in Price's first year.

The Jefferson Standard Building

Price also understood the value of confidence. Insurance companies operate on trust and stability. People like to identify their financial institutions with impressive buildings that inspire confidence that the company can be trusted with their hard-earned money and, indeed, their financial futures.

In the early 1920s, Jefferson Standard continued to operate out of several floors of a building in downtown Greensboro owned by Dixie Fire Insurance. As the company grew, it overflowed into several adjoining buildings and storefronts. Finally, in 1922, Price and the board of directors decided it was time to build a new headquarters. Price was determined that Jefferson Standard would build a headquarters that befitted its position as one of the fastest growing insurance companies in the state, and the company laid plans for one of the most ambitious office buildings in the South.

For its site, Jefferson Standard chose the city's most sacred place: the intersection of Market and Elm Streets on Courthouse Square, where court had been held for more than 110 years. Architect Charles C. Hartman was hired to design a new headquarters. The building he envisioned combined classical, Romanesque, Gothic, and art deco architecture. It had two towers rising 17 stories above the ground. The north and west sides were left plain to accommodate future growth.

Ground was broken in 1922 and construction began. More than 3,000 tons of steel, nine train carloads of granite, 37 train carloads of terracotta and 111 train carloads full of brick were ultimately used.[2] Signs at the construction site advertised it as "a real building for progressive folks in a thriving city. Rent now." Amazingly, when it opened in 1923 at a cost of $2.5 million, it was entirely paid for because Julian Price didn't believe in debt.

In 1922, ground was broken for a new Jefferson Standard headquarters building in downtown Greensboro. The 17-story building opened in 1923 and remained in operation 80 years later.

The new building was a wonder of modern construction technology. It had its own systems for telephone, transportation, fire, police, engineering, and street-cleaning. The elevators traveled at 600 feet a minute to the top of the building from which Pilot Mountain, 70 miles away, was visible on a clear day.

The elegant building attracted attention from across the state and the South. It stood "looming large on the skyline," according to company literature, and most observers agreed. Will Rogers is said to have remarked from a local stage that Greensboro was the first place he had seen a sky-

JULIAN PRICE

JULIAN PRICE WAS BORN NOVEMBER 25, 1867, and grew up during the Reconstruction period. He attended rural public schools and learned at an early age to work hard and make the most of any assets at hand. One of his first jobs was cutting and selling wood to the Southern Railway for wood-burning locomotives. At the age of 20, he became a telegraph operator and dispatcher for the railway. His next job was selling snuff as a traveling salesman for the American Tobacco Company. In 1905, at the age of 38, he moved to Greensboro and began his life insurance career at the Greensboro Life Insurance Company.

By 1909, Price had become a secretary and manager of Greensboro Life, and with the consolidation of Jefferson Standard and Greensboro Life in 1912, Price became vice president and agency manager of Jefferson Standard.

It was an age of powerfully spoken men: Woodrow Wilson was president of the United States when Price became company president in 1919, and Price was of the same mold. Even as a young man he had a presence about him, a spark and wit that impressed those around him. He was known for his shrewd business instincts and personal style. He was an immaculate dresser, carrying gold-tipped canes and wearing fedora hats. Price's leadership extended outside of Jefferson Standard to his community and state. In 1920 he was elected to the Greensboro City Council, where he served for seven years.

Throughout his leadership at Jefferson Standard, he proved eminently quotable. Some of the quotes attributed to Price over the years include:

Stay out of debt. If you don't owe any money, you're able to look a man in the eye and tell him to go to Hell.

I like a fellow with his shoulders back and his head up. A fellow who looks like he is going somewhere.

If you wait until you're sure you're right, you'll lose many opportunities. My aim is to be right 51 percent of the time, and if I succeed in doing that, I'm well satisfied.

scraper go up in the middle of farmland. The *Greensboro Daily News* reported that the structure was the "greatest office building in North Carolina." It would surely usher in a new age of commerce in Greensboro, the newspaper said. Indeed, it quickly filled with shops and professionals, including doctors, dentists, and lawyers; a barber shop; a smoke shop; a railway ticket office; and a top-floor restaurant. Jefferson Standard would gradually expand into the whole building.

In 1923, Rogers' comment that the building was in the middle of farmland wasn't far-fetched. The Jefferson Standard building was the only skyscraper between Washington, D.C., and Atlanta. It was also the most elegant. Home office employees and field men were honorary members of the company's City Club, located on the 17th floor. The City Club offered fine dining and dancing.[3]

Employees also enjoyed membership privileges at Jefferson Standard Country Club, on a wooded knoll about seven miles from downtown. The country club grew to include 500 acres, a spacious clubhouse, a six-acre swimming lake with a sandy beach, a 25-acre boating and fishing lake, tennis and badminton courts, and picnic areas.

Solid Growth

By the time the Jefferson Standard building opened, America was in full-blown transition into the modern era. Throughout the early 1920s, technologies that had once been rare or prohibitively expensive began to proliferate. Consumer goods such as wristwatches, cigarette lighters, cameras, and washing machines were suddenly affordable for most middle-income Americans. By 1920, there were about 10,000 movie screens in America, whereas in 1905 there had been only one. Similarly, radio was spreading rapidly. By the end of 1922, more than 500 radio stations were broadcasting to about three million listeners, and the first radio commercial had aired. By 1920, more than eight million cars were registered in America—a number that would increase almost four-fold by the end of the decade.

It seemed fitting that Jefferson Standard would welcome an era of such prosperity from the commanding heights of a new building. In 1923, the company achieved its second $100 million of insurance in force. To keep employees focused, Julian Price offered five dollars to the employee who submitted the best article on "My Idea of Personal Success." The President's Club, also called the Julian Price Club, was established to recognize each month's highest-selling agents.

One of the first to attain this elite status was Albert Lee Smith, who began working for Jefferson Standard in 1911 in Birmingham, Alabama, accepting eggs, vegetables, and hams for premiums and setting up shop wherever he could, including in an undertaker's parlor. In 1982, at the age of 92, Smith still had a company contract. By then, he had sold more than $44 million of insurance.

"Insurance is next to preaching with me," Smith said. "I've seen the good it can do for a family. If the customer lives a long time, he gets his money back. If not, his family will have money to put food in the kids' mouths and pay off the mortgage."[4]

Jefferson Standard maintained its torrid pace of growth through the middle of the decade. In October 1924, the company reinsured the business of the Carolina Mutual Life Insurance Company of Raleigh, amounting to $870,000 of new business.[5] By 1925, Jefferson Standard was the 35th largest company of its kind in the country, insuring more than 40,000 North Carolinians for $90 million.

In 1927, Julian Price turned sixty and celebrated one of the best years in Jefferson Standard's history. To reward employees for their efforts, he recommended a 5 percent salary increase, which the board of directors unanimously approved. By 1928, the company ranked 31st in size among 300 competitors and operated in twenty-six states, the District of Columbia, and Puerto Rico. It employed 211 people in its home office and boasted $340 million worth of insurance in force.[6]

A Confident Pilot

Across town, Southern Life & Trust headed into the 1920s with the same sense of gravity as Jefferson Standard. Although the company was writing new policies at a rapid pace, a high mortality rate translated into $1.6 million in death benefits. This money was used to support bereaved spouses, feed and educate parentless children, and sustain families that lost a breadwinner in the hard years between 1918 and 1920. Writing to employees, President A. W. McAlister said, "We enter 1920 with a solemn sense of our responsibility, and a confidence based on tests endured and difficulties overcome."[7]

To keep the sales momentum, Southern Life & Trust announced a weekly business target of $350,000 in 1920 and exhorted its agents and customers to save more money. "A half dollar a day poorly spent consumes the income of an investment fund of $3,650," said an article in the *Pilot*, a

Pilot Life Insurance Co - 1928

The office staff gathers at Pilot in 1928. By this time, the company had a Weekly Premium Department, in addition to offering life, health, and accident insurance.

company newsletter. Research indicated that 82 of every 100 men in New York State died with no income-producing estate. As a result, out of every 100 widows, 18 enjoyed a comfortable lifestyle, 47 worked to support themselves, and 35 were left destitute and dependent on charity.[8]

The company also continued its practice of sending health care professionals on rounds to visit policy holders. The flu epidemic had deeply scarred the country, coming out of seemingly nowhere to kill hundreds of thousands and receding just as abruptly and mysteriously.

As it contended with the twin tragedies of sickness and war, Southern Life also endured a boll weevil epidemic in the agricultural South. These insects devastated cotton fields, leaving farmers unable to pay their life insurance premiums.

Farmers tried various deterrents, including poisoning the bugs with calcium arsenate (too expensive for the average farmer) and zapping the weevils with electrical currents (99 percent of the boll weevils survived).

Still McAlister sought to grow, working to offer "the largest service to the largest number." At the company convention in Niagara Falls in July 1920, McAlister announced a new organization and sales structure. Southern Life established an Ordinary Health and Accident Division and an Intermediate

Division, which served industry, including the many textile mills in the area.[9] A new Weekly Premium Department sold a policy that combined life, health, and accident insurance in one contract at affordable rates.

The Weekly Premium Department would evolve into Pilot's home service division. The idea of weekly premium insurance, or industrial insurance, began in England, where insurance companies approached employers about offering basic insurance to their workers, many of whom were low-paid assembly workers. As the name implies, the premiums were collected every week by roving agents, who sometimes walked through small villages or even waited at factory gates.

In 1920, as the new departments were introduced, Southern Life wrote $20.13 million in ordinary insurance and $9,330 in accident and health insurance. Despite this success, the next year would prove to be one of the most challenging years in Southern Life & Trust's history. The cotton market, still reeling from the boll weevil epidemic, suffered through a local drought and yet more farmers were pressured to default on their insurance.

In 1923, A. W. McAlister combined Southern Life's annual convention with that of the McAlister, Vaughn, & Scales General Agency, another of his business ventures. "In this way," McAlister announced in the company newsletter, "the members of the two branches of the Pilot organization will have an opportunity to become acquainted with each other."[10] The move itself wasn't significant, but for one telling reason: It was one of the first times that Southern Life & Trust was officially referred to as "the Pilot," the name by which most locals knew it.

In 1924, Southern Life & Trust announced its third name change, one that didn't come as a surprise to anyone. At the time of its founding, 21 years before, company officers had chosen "Southern" to show the company's roots. There weren't many Southern companies around. By the early 1920s, however, more than 30 competitors used "South" or "Southern" in their names. To distinguish the company, officers announced that from henceforth, Southern Life & Trust would be called Pilot Life Insurance Company. The company's new logo featured a raincoatted skipper behind a ship's wheel, with Pilot Mountain pictured inside the wheel. The slogan became "Pilot to protection since 1903."[11]

A Local Campus

In the mid-1920s, Pilot Life grew quickly, capitalizing on opportunities as they arose. The company had expanded beyond individual life insurance

to offer accident, health, and industrial insurance. By 1927, Pilot Life had amassed assets of almost $10 million.[12] That year, President A. W. McAlister wrote that Pilot's strengths included "the ability to visualize opportunity, making the most of it by untiring industry, undismayed by any obstacle; the careful selection of men, training them from the ground up . . . and the full recognition of merit of suggestion, even if it comes from the office boy."

Like his counterpart at Jefferson Standard, McAlister recognized that it was time for Pilot to find new quarters. Whereas Jefferson Standard headed for the heart of the city, McAlister's instincts took him in another direction: the country. He envisioned creating an entire campus devoted to Pilot Life, one that included recreation facilities, business, and even upscale housing.

This desire fit perfectly with McAlister's experience, temperament, and philosophies. In 1911, together with partners Alfred M. Scales and R. G. Vaughn, McAlister had developed Irving Park, a residential community of stately homes. Scales was a former governor (1885–1889) who had reached the rank of

brigadier general in the Confederate army[13] and enjoyed success in real estate, including selling the O. Henry Drugstore site for a price that amounted to $3,000 a square foot.[14] McAlister had also created Greensboro's first golf course, which later became Greensboro Country Club.

Moreover, McAlister believed that corporations were duty bound to care for their employees, just as they were obligated to make a good return for their shareholders. His career and his public life were marked by moralism, temperance, and community service. For McAlister, it was only natural that a successful company like Pilot Life would return that success to its employees by affording them a pleasant place to live and play, as well as a stable place to work.

Right: The Pilot logo became a well-known sight throughout North Carolina and the entire South. It featured Pilot Mountain inside the wheel of a ship's pilot.

Below: Pilot Life home office employees gather in 1930 on the lawn of Sedgefield, Pilot's new headquarters, built in 1927 and 1928.

Above: When Pilot President A. W. McAlister began to develop Sedgefield, he drew upon his experience with Irving Park, an upscale housing community he and his partners had built.

Below: Jefferson Standard home-office employees pose on the roof of the Jefferson Standard building in downtown Greensboro. Their building dominated the city's skyline.

Thus, in 1923 McAlister bought 3,660 rolling acres between Greenboro and High Point, dubbing the property "Sedgefield." It was divided into lots, and portions of it were sold by Southern Real Estate for development. In 1927 the Sedgefield Inn opened as a luxury resort hotel.

The crown jewel of Sedgefield, however, was the realization of McAlister's vision for a new headquarters. In 1927, company officials made a pilgrimage to Pilot Mountain to retrieve a large block of granite for the cornerstone of the complex. The official ground breaking took place on June 21, 1927.

By 1928, Pilot Life was ready to move into its new headquarters. The main building encompassed three stories plus a basement and a loft in thirty-five thousand square feet. The impressive brick building was a careful replication of the governor's mansion built in 1767 in New Bern, North Carolina. The architects were Zantsinger, Borie and Madary of Philadelphia, and Harry Barton of Greensboro. For landscaping, McAlister employed R. B. Cridland, the same architect who had developed Irving Park.

SEDGEFIELD~GREENSBORO
NORTH CAROLINA

A Sedgefield Inn brochure advertising the hotel, located on the same rolling property where Pilot Life was building its ambitious new headquarters and residential community.

The complex's eastern building, with 12,000 square feet, housed the Pilot family of affiliated fire insurance companies as well as the industrial weekly premium, accident, and health divisions of the Pilot Life Insurance Company. The complex was named after David Parks Fackler, the company's first actuary and an internationally recognized authority on insurance.

Sedgefield offered a host of benefits to Pilot Life employees. There was a cafeteria that seated 156 and operated on an honor system: After eating, employees filled out their own checks. There was also a medical office equipped with "every modern appliance for the scientific study of the human body from the life insurance standpoint." A large automatic document carrier moved through the entire complex, distributing business papers. Office space for the underwriters allowed for plenty of sunlight and fresh air through the windows. Sparkling water bubbled from a 339-foot well, and a comfortable lounge in the Commons building offered a handsomely decorated place to relax. The building had no time clocks, as the honor system had always been used "with excellent results."[15]

Pilot Life employees quickly warmed to Sedgefield, and the campus would remain a beloved company fixture until the late 1980s.

Pulling Together

In 1927, Pilot Life and Jefferson Standard had both carved out respectable niches in the insurance industry. They were direct but friendly competitors, both run by powerful personalities and deeply entrenched in the North Carolina soil from which they had sprung.

At Jefferson Standard, Julian Price pushed the company into new regions and ever greater financial goals. He believed that Jefferson Standard should stick with the life insurance it knew best and expand into new regions. Thus he had moved Jefferson Standard to exotic locales like Cuba and Puerto Rico at a time when few American corporations were venturing outside of their regions, much less the continental United States.

At Pilot, A. W. McAlister sought growth through diversification. Pilot Life steadily grew its organization chart to include industrial, group life, accident, and health insurance, as well as ordinary life insurance. This diversification, like Jefferson Standard's expansion, worked, and the company grew quickly. Like Jefferson, Pilot had also developed a personality, one sculpted by McAlister. In 1927, this personality and its code of ethics were adopted by a group called the McAlister Clan.

The McAlister Clan, which included company officers, pledged responsibility to clients and policy holders, to the company, and to themselves.

Background: An aerial view of the Sedgefield campus, taken several decades after the building was constructed. This beloved campus was the headquarters of Pilot Life until the late 1980s.

Opposite: The 1927 ground-breaking event at Sedgefield. Pilot Life employees gathered (larger photo) to watch the first shovelfuls of dirt be turned by company officials (smaller photo).

Right: A. W. McAlister helps lay the cornerstone for the Sedgefield building. This stone was native granite quarried from nearby Pilot Mountain.

Top right: A poster advertising the ground-breaking for Sedgefield.

McAlister sits at his desk in his new office shortly after the Sedgefield building was completed. The new campus fit his philosophy of corporate benevolence.

Like previous writings from McAlister, the group's charter proclaimed the inherent goodness in life insurance, saying that life insurance was a "great humanitarian service and the arch enemy of misery, want and economic loss." Members of the McAlister Clan aspired to be "wise in love . . . a wholesome spirit, my heart in the right place, attuned to the divine music of truth and love, with life expressing loyalty to God and goodwill to man."[16]

For validation of its methods, Pilot needed look no further than its bottom line. In 1919, the company had about $48 million worth of insurance in force; by the end of 1928, the figure had grown to almost $100 million.

Located in the same town, with similar records of success and led by similar personalities, Jefferson Standard and Pilot Life were naturally attracted to one another. In many ways, they were complementary, each active in a slightly different area of the same industry. In 1927, ever the astute investor, Julian Price directed Jefferson Standard to buy a chunk of Pilot Life stock. At this point, Jefferson Standard was a passive investor, but the two companies were beginning a relationship that would last for seven decades and beyond.

The Depression Begins

By the time Jefferson Standard made its investment in Pilot Life, the two companies could look back with satisfaction on the years just passed. Jefferson Standard had more than $200 million of insurance in force, and Pilot would pass the $100 million mark in 1929. Unfortunately, other forces were in motion that year that would quickly undermine the financial stability of the United States economy. Throughout the 1920s, the U.S. economy had grown astonishingly fast, leading

THE CREED OF THE "McALISTER CLAN"

I BELIEVE IN THE INSTITUTION OF LIFE insurance, in the Pilot Life Insurance Company and in the dignity of my profession.

As a life insurance underwriter I recognize a threefold responsibility—to my clients and policy holders, to my Company, to myself. I believe that success is to be measured not in volume of business alone but in the conscientious discharge of the many daily duties by which it is my privilege to aid in extending the great humanitarian service of life insurance, the arch enemy of misery, want and economic loss.

To my clients I owe unerring and unselfish council based on expert knowledge of insurance and the affairs of men, a sympathetic understanding of their problems and their aspirations, and relentless zeal and patient endeavor in my efforts to sell them adequate and intelligent protection. To my policy holders I owe my services at all times without stint or thought of self. With a full realization that a lapsed policy is always an economic waste and too often is a cruel tragedy, I believe that if I contribute willfully to that tragedy or waste through ignorance, pre-meditation, or indifference I am unworthy of a place in the life underwriting profession.

To my Company I owe unreserved loyalty and allegiance, expressing my appreciation of able service rendered, exercising poise and self-restraint in all trying situations, and constantly sensing the community of interest of the field and home office forces in unswerving adherence to sound underwriting.

To myself I owe a sound body—the physical ability to work without handicap, with zest, with tenacity, and with effectiveness; a contented mind free from worry, anxiety, fear—prudent in financing, wise in love, carrying a good conscience regardless of cost, counting nothing worthwhile which does not bring happiness as an essential part of success; a wholesome spirit, my heart in the right place, attuned to the divine music of truth and love, reaching out to the plains of the earth, with the life expressing loyalty to God and goodwill to man.

—Signed by charter members
September 8, 1927

some economists to speculate that the country had entered a period of permanent growth. Stock market gains were matched by real estate gains, and investors made wild profits.

By 1929, however, the fundamentals were shaky—productivity was declining, new housing starts were falling off, manufacturing activity was slowing, and the crucial agricultural industry was suffering from an unprecedented drought. At the time, no one seemed to notice, and the stock market continued its upward spiral, venturing into a realm that could later be described only as fantasy.

Finally, on October 29, 1929, the bill came due. That day, the stock market fell a total of 13 percent, or 43 points. By the end of the month, the New York Stock Exchange had lost 37 percent of its value. This staggering drop was the first sobering sign of the oncoming Great Depression. Between 1929 and 1932, Americans' personal incomes declined by more than half, from $82 million to $40 million. Unemployment reached 25 percent, and commodity prices dropped by half. Farmers declared bankruptcy by the hundreds, and local banks were driven out of business. In the first three years of the Depression, more than 9,000 banks closed, factories and mines shut their doors, and entire towns were abandoned as the American social and financial system fell to its knees.[17]

In March 1933, in response to the failure of the banking system, newly elected President Franklin D. Roosevelt declared a three-day nationwide bank holiday. Before a bank reopened, it had to meet strict capital requirements that Roosevelt issued. As a result, every bank in Greensboro stayed locked, most of them forever.

With no surviving banks in town, Guilford County script was issued and generally accepted as a medium of exchange.[18] Jefferson Standard leaders, however, recognized this was only a temporary fix, and they moved to open a new bank that fit Roosevelt's stringent capital requirements. In 1933, Jefferson Standard, together with the Reconstruction Finance Corporation, organized the

Security National Bank. The company also founded the Greensboro National Bank, which later became a part of Bank of America. Pilot contributed its share, investing in the Guilford National Bank.[19]

Other than opening banks, the two companies reacted differently to the challenging time. Pilot Life slipped below its impressive $100 million milestone in 1932 and 1933, although it regained the amount in 1934. At the same time, Pilot Life's investment portfolio was severely damaged by falling real estate values. The company had invested much of its money in the real estate market through first mortgages to homeowners. The high default rate wreaked havoc with Pilot's mortgage portfolio.

The downturn would soon affect the other companies in the Pilot family, including Pilot Fire Insurance, George Washington Fire Insurance, and Greensboro Fire Insurance. The same set of officers led all these companies, and A. W. McAlister held important positions in each. The companies also shared offices and annual conventions, and Pilot Life owned a considerable amount of stock in each company. In 1931, in response to the deteriorating economy, all three of the fire insurance companies were divested.[20] At the same time, Pilot Life sold its health and accident business to the Inter-Ocean Casualty Company, of Cincinnati, Ohio.

Opposite: Scenes from Pilot Life Insurance's annual outings at Pilot Mountain. The company took all its employees to the mountain by train for picnicking, hiking, and bonding.

Jefferson Standard Life Insurance Co.
Convention New Orleans
Feb. 16-17-18, 1931

Harcol
N.O. La.

Jefferson Buys Pilot Life

Above: Jefferson Standard agents and employees pose during the company's 1931 convention in New Orleans, where the mayor presented company officers with keys to the city.

Opposite: This letter announced the acquisition of Pilot Life by Jefferson Standard. Each Pilot Life employee was assured the company would remain a separate and proud entity.

In contrast to Pilot's struggles, Jefferson Standard steadily increased its insurance in force, partly because of the company's broad diversification. In August 1930, Jefferson Standard offices in Asheville, North Carolina, Huntington, West Virginia, and Atlanta, Georgia showed month-over-month increases of 30 percent, 2 percent, and 10 percent, respectively.

In February 1931, the company gathered in New Orleans for an agent convention at which Jefferson Standard—almost alone among American companies—celebrated its success. As the company officers arrived in town, the mayor even presented them with the keys to the city.[21] Jefferson's growth streak continued: In November 1931, the company

set a record for monthly business, and on November 26, it set a daily record of slightly more than $2 million in new business.

Around the same time, Jefferson Standard President Julian Price announced that Jefferson Standard had purchased a controlling interest in Pilot Life, thus consummating a relationship that

PILOT LIFE INSURANCE COMPANY

HOME OFFICE
GREENSBORO, NORTH CAROLINA

A.W.McALISTER, PRESIDENT.
R.G.VAUGHN, VICE PRESIDENT.
H.S.RICHARDSON, VICE PREST.
H.B.GUNTER, VICE PRESIDENT
ARTHUR WATT, SECY.& ACTUARY.
H.F.STARR, M.D.,MEDICAL DIRECTOR.
T.D.BLAIR, AGENCY MANAGER
T.D.DUPUY, TREASURER.

December 3, 1930

Dear Piloteer:

You received yesterday President McAlister's
letter announcing that the Jefferson Standard
now owns the majority of the capital stock of
the Pilot. Let me call your attention to his
statement "The Jefferson Standard has the utmost friendliness for the Pilot ------ that the
Pilot is to continue as a separate and independent organization at its present location -----
and that I am to continue as President of the
Company."

Also the statement of President Julian Price of
the Jefferson that "It is our plan and purpose
for the Pilot Life Insurance Company to continue
to operate as it does now as a separate and independent organization at its present location.
There can be no conflict of interests ------ I
confidently expect both companies to achieve bigger and better things."

These statements of policy mean that we are facing
tremendously increased opportunities, that the
separate identity of the Pilot Life Insurance Company is to be a permanent thing, and that we can
lead the way in the biggest life insurance picture
in the South, so let's buckle in and show President
McAlister during the month of December that we are
with him to a man by piling up a whale of a business for the month.

Write Mr. "Mac" a letter and tell him about your
loyalty if you want to, but you will make him feel
still better if you say it with applications. Let's
make December an informal "Loyalty Month."

Yours very truly,

T.D.Blair

TDB:RC

Agency Manager.

Left: Charles Gold became president at Pilot after McAlister retired, just after Pilot was purchased by Jefferson Standard.

Right: In 1934, after Gold died in a hunting accident, Emry C. Green, a former Jefferson Standard employee, was named president of Pilot Life. He managed the company through the difficult years of the Great Depression.

had begun four years before. In no way was this considered a hostile takeover. In announcing the acquisition, McAlister declared, "I am assured by the executives of Jefferson Standard Life Insurance Company that they have no other than a purpose of the utmost friendliness towards Pilot Life . . . and that Pilot Life Insurance Company shall continue as a separate organization . . . and that I continue as president." McAlister predicted the change would generate "a generous rivalry, a rivalry between friends, and ought to stimulate us to our very best."[22]

In the first months after the acquisition, Jefferson Standard invested $600,000 in Pilot Life. In March 1932, despite his announcement, A. W. McAlister, then 69 years old, announced his retirement after 25 years of service. The company had $13 million in assets and $86 million of insurance in force. Charles W. Gold, one of the original investors and founders of Jefferson Standard, was named Pilot's third president.

Shortly after assuming his new office, Gold wrote company shareholders, acknowledging the difficult business conditions. He pointed out that after nearly doubling its insurance in force between 1921 and 1926, Pilot had posted only a 20 percent increase between 1926 and 1931. Moreover, many of the company's policy holders had taken loans against their policies to relieve the financial strain of the Depression. Gold reminded policy holders that borrowing against their policies amounted to "a loan from your widow" and advised them to make strict plans for repayment.

Whether Charles Gold would have been an effective Depression-era leader at Pilot would never be tested. In September 1933, he was killed in a hunting accident after serving less than two years.

A New President

After the accident, a 70-year-old McAlister agreed to return to the company until a new president could be located. The search wouldn't take long. In 1934, 35-year-old Emry C. Green was appointed the fourth president of Pilot Life. Unlike McAlister, who had grown up in the Pilot organization, Green had been with the company only a year, joining as executive vice president in 1933. He had come up through Jefferson Standard, joining the filing department in 1922 at 22.[23]

Green was native to North Carolina. He was born and raised in Weldon before attending college at the Georgia Institute of Technology and serving in the military. In his early twenties, Green was making the relatively princely sum of $300 a month playing professional baseball, working in the local post office, and teaching high school athletics. His multifaceted career was interrupted when a

Opposite: Even into the 1930s, Pilot Life and Jefferson Standard continued to focus their advertising on the benefit of buying life insurance locally. By this time, the companies were pumping millions of investment dollars into the local economy, in addition to promoting golf.

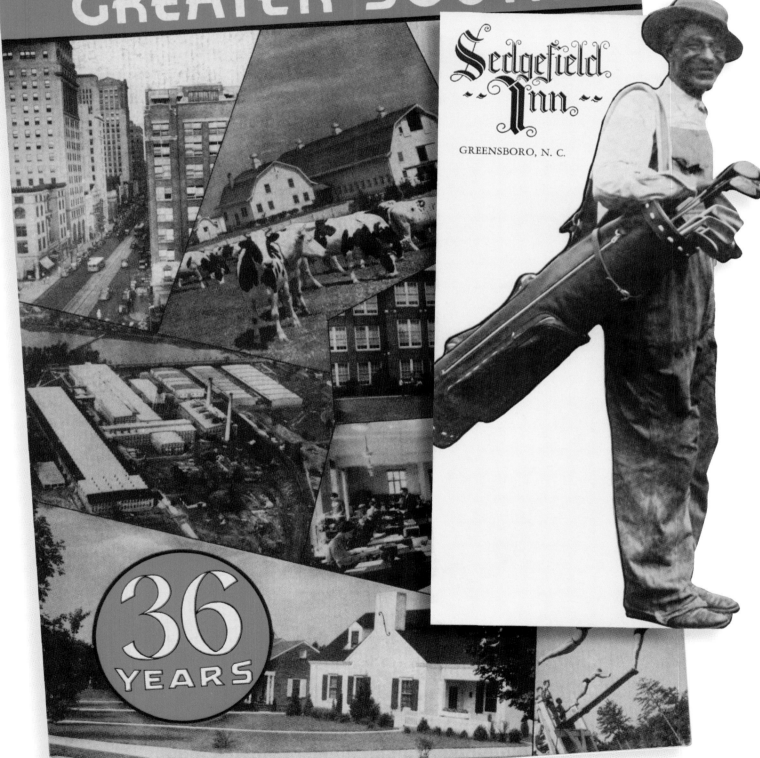

HELPING BUILD THE GREATER SOUTH

36 YEARS

Sedgefield Inn

GREENSBORO, N. C.

The employee executive committee of the Jefferson Standard Club in the 1930s. During that era, Jefferson Standard was one of the few successful insurance companies in the country.

Jefferson Standard personnel officer offered Green $60 a week to join the filing department. Green accepted the job.

In 1934, as he assumed control over Pilot, Green counted on the support of his seasoned board, which included A. W. McAlister as chairman, Julian Price, and Julius C. Smith as general counsel. At the end of his first year, Pilot reported an increase of $3.3 million of insurance in force, for a total once again more than $100 million. The company had added more than 10,000 policy holders over the year and boasted total assets of $14.26 million.[24]

Charting A Course through the Thirties

Emry Green would not dramatically change Pilot Life's strategic direction, instead focusing on saving costs wherever possible. An in-house memo in 1934 expressed concern over communications and travel expenses. Noting that phone call expenses were mounting—an extravagant $80 monthly for the Ordinary department, he suggested that a letter could often take the place of a call. Trains cost less than personal automobiles for certain home office trips.

He also continued McAlister's tradition of upholding the highest professional standards. During one departmental meeting, he announced a ban on whistling and singing at work, based on the notion that these behaviors were unprofessional.

Gradually, Pilot's business began to expand once again. The company's policy holder mortality rate, all important to an insurance company, averaged about half of what was expected in 1934 while the dollar amount of the average policy continued to increase, rising to $1,500 by the end of the year.[25] Sales also increased: The important Weekly Premium department showed a $1 million gain in insurance in force in the first quarter of 1935.

The financial turnaround also resulted from Pilot's strategy to reduce its reliance on real estate and buy discounted state, county, and municipal bonds. The 1936 financial statement showed assets of nearly $16.5 million, an additional 22,600 new policy holders, and the largest amount of insurance in force in Pilot's history.[26] By 1937, Pilot had broken three of its own records: It had achieved the largest gain of insurance in force, the largest increase in assets, and the largest volume of paid business in any single year.[27]

"The company has long been ably managed in the interest of its policy holders and the results achieved are above the average for the business," said *Best's Life Insurance Reports*. "In our opinion it has ample margin for contingencies."[28]

In 1939, Pilot focused on stability, service, and quality and continued to center its advertising on the central theme of serving southerners. Green boasted that 97.5 percent of company assets were invested in the South. Here, the company benefited from a demographic quirk: The southern states were home to a larger percentage of young people than any other area of the country. As a result, for more than two decades Pilot had an outstandingly low mortality rate of 50.7 percent, compared to 58.9 percent for the ten largest insurance companies in the country.

In addition to homegrown investments, Pilot could claim a homegrown clientele. With $135 million of insurance in force, it had never reinsured another company. Of the $20 million it had invested in securities, more than a quarter was guaranteed by the federal government. Pilot had paid an average of 4.6 percent interest for the previous decade.

The Standard Picture

Although Pilot Life was owned by Jefferson Standard throughout the 1930s, the companies remained separate operations, each experiencing

The Jefferson Standard employee lounge. The company's trademark building was the defining feature of the downtown Greensboro skyline.

the Great Depression in different ways. More geographically diversified and larger, Jefferson Standard had an easier time in the early 1930s than Pilot did. In 1932, the company paid $4.5 million to policy holders while writing $18.5 million in business in the first six months of the year. In a company document published in 1932, Price wrote, "The dream of a richer, better, fuller life for those who have come under the influence of Jefferson has been realized . . . we look back with thankfulness and forward to the shining future."[29] By 1933, 1,000 Jefferson Standard agents had offices in 25 states.

Jefferson Standard's success during the Depression allowed it to expand its product offerings to attract new business. In 1932 and 1933, the company announced a Salary Savings Plan, a form of employee pension plan in a day when pension plans were rare and Social Security had not yet been created. More than 300 companies signed up in the program's first year. Under the plan, employers deducted a specified monthly amount from their employees' pay checks and sent the money to Jefferson Standard for investment. The accounts had no cash value or loan value until the second premium had been paid.

In 1933, the company introduced a "Dixie Special" policy that was designed to help cash-strapped southerners. This policy offered a graduated premium that started low and increased until it leveled out in the sixth year. The first annual premium for a $5,000 policy at age 35 was $44.65.

In mid-1933, Julian Price announced that Jefferson Standard had enjoyed the best six months in its history. Yet more change was coming. At that year's semiannual meeting, Emry Green, the company's secretary, resigned his position at Jefferson Standard and moved to Pilot as executive vice president—soon to be president. In his place, Joseph M. Bryan was elected company secretary. The son-in-law of Julian Price, Bryan was a larger-than-life figure with a booming voice who was destined to remain a fixture at Jefferson Standard for many decades to come.

In conjunction with these moves, President Julian Price pointed out that a special fund of $800,000 had been set aside to cover depreciation of the company's real estate investments and other losses attributed to the ongoing Depression. He also noted that the company showed an operating profit, owned no bank stock, and had borrowed no money. "The capital, surplus and contingent reserves, totaling approximately $4 million, constitute by any yardstick ample protection for policy holders," he said.[30]

That same year, perhaps for the first time, a female face gazed out of the company publication *The Jeffersonian* from a spot in the company newsletter usually reserved for male agents. Baylor-educated Mrs. John C. Fortune, who had come to work for the company on July 3, 1923, was profiled as the "First Lady of the Dallas Agency." Another female agent who regularly appeared in the company magazine during the thirties was Mrs. E. T. Matthews, of the Memphis agency, who often achieved a 100 percent renewal in business. In the January 1935 issue of the company's publication, *The Jeffersonian*, Matthews explained her key to success: "Sell a need, not a policy. Work all day, every day, in a systematic and enthusiastic way."

By 1935, Jefferson Standard had been in business for almost a third of a century and had enjoyed great success under Julian Price's steady leadership. More people bought Jefferson Standard policies in 1935 than in any other year in the company history, totaling more than 150,000 policies of up to $250,000. Jefferson representatives operated in 24 states, the District of Columbia, and Puerto Rico.

The company's investment decisions also proved superior. Between 1935 and 1937, Jefferson Standard led all major life insurance companies in net interest earned on invested assets. In every year since its founding in 1907, it had paid 5 percent interest on funds held in trust for policy holders and beneficiaries—a record unequaled by any other life insurance company in the United States.

By the end of the 1930s, Jefferson Standard had achieved $400 million of insurance in force. In 1938, capital was increased by 100 percent to $2 million, and par value of the stock, which had started at $50, increased to $100. Jefferson Standard averaged between 4,000 and 5,000 policy holders and about $10 million of insurance in force

Opposite: Julian and Ethel Clay Price. The two were generous benefactors in the state of North Carolina, giving money to fund parks, churches, and buildings.

in each state in which it operated. In North Carolina alone it had 50,000 policy holders. More than 6,500 Southern Bell Telephone employees were on Jefferson Standard's Salary Savings Plan.[31]

Finally, in the late 1930s, the company purchased a controlling interest in the local Gate City Life Insurance Company, again expanding its influence and reach into Greensboro's once more thriving life insurance industry.

Ralph Price

Julian Price had run Jefferson Standard since 1920. Much of the company's success was owed to his vision to push sales, his prudence in guiding the company's investment portfolio, and his appetite for expansion. Yet he was approaching 70, and it

Julian Price gathers for cake with a group of home office employees. Miss Mary, a beloved employee who stayed in close touch with the field agents, stands to his left.

was clear that a succession plan was called for. In July 1937, the board of directors elected his son, Ralph Price, to the executive committee. Ralph Price was already a board member and vice president. A year later, Ralph succeeded A. R. Perkins as head of the all-important Jefferson Standard Agency Department.

As he set about grooming his son to lead the company, Julian Price could take great pride in the institution he had helped build and the legacy he was leaving. He was one of the most well known men in North Carolina, even among those who did not buy insurance. At his direction, Jefferson Standard had invested almost $30 million directly into the state. Carl Goerch, a writer for *The State* magazine, gave a radio broadcast every Saturday morning in the late 1930s in which he quizzed passersby and audience members. Goerch gave a dollar for each correct answer. Through the years he handed out several hundred dollars to those who correctly answered the question, "Who is Julian Price?"

Price, however, looked askance at the idea that Jefferson Standard's success was due to any personal trait of his. "It's a left-handed compliment," he said. "To tell the truth, it's really a reflection against me—to think that during the length of time I've been connected with the Jefferson Standard I have been unable to build up an organization that would function smoothly regardless of who dropped out of it."[32]

The Coming of World War II

By the late 1930s, both companies had changed a great deal. Because of its exposure to the real estate market, Pilot Life had experienced the Great Depression more acutely than had Jefferson Standard. In the early 1930s, the Pilot family of companies was broken up, with the fire insurance companies going to competitors, and Pilot had dropped certain lines of insurance. The setbacks, however, were temporary. By the mid-1930s, Pilot Life was growing quickly again. Jefferson Standard, on the other hand, maintained a steady, enviable record of growth throughout the worst of the Depression.

The companies had changed in other, more fundamental ways. By the end of the 1930s, Pilot Life was a wholly owned subsidiary of Jefferson Standard, although the companies continued to function as independent entities. Both companies had also experienced leadership changes. A. W. McAlister, the longtime leader of Pilot, retired shortly after Jefferson Standard bought the company; he was succeeded by Emry Green, an import from Jefferson Standard. Similarly, at Jefferson Standard, longtime leader Julian Price was on the verge of retiring and was grooming his son to take over the company. The two companies were fortunate to have enjoyed such strong leadership during a dark time in the country's history.

The dark days had not yet ended, however. The Depression that hit the United States was part of a worldwide economic stagnation, partly driven by the crushing aftermath of World War I. Between 1919 and 1939, the world suffered through a prolonged period of nationalism, restricted trade, and high tariffs. Germany suffered under the onerous terms of the Treaty of Versailles, which demanded war reparations from the ravaged country. By the late 1930s, the currency situation in Germany was so bad that wheelbarrows of German marks were essentially worthless. Into this unstable, unhappy void stepped a menace of unprecedented proportion in the person of Adolf Hitler, the nationalistic, charismatic, and racist leader of the Nazi Party. Hitler sought to rebuild German pride through carefully orchestrated parades and events, a forbidden military buildup, and military conquest. He found an ally in Imperial Japan and began to plot his domination of Europe. Before long, Austria and Czechoslovakia had been consumed by Germany.

On September 1, 1939, Hitler finally went one step too far. His forces attacked Poland, conquering the country in a devastating, high-speed, mechanized form of ground war that became known as blitzkrieg. Stunned, Britain and France declared war as the German war machine turned its appetite westward. Across the Pacific, meanwhile, Japan had steadily expanded its empire to include much of mainland China, oil fields in Indochina, and huge swaths of Southeast Asia.

As it had at the outset of World War I, the United States maintained an uneasy neutrality. But with the war going badly for Europe and China, it seemed to many that the United States would soon be called upon once again to take up arms in defense of Europe and its allies. In September 1939, only weeks after the German blitzkrieg in Poland, Julian Price sent a letter to Jefferson Standard associates discussing the possibility of U.S. involvement in the war. "The effect of the war abroad is certain to be harmful," he wrote; "however, I see no reason why we should not be able to continue our work in a normal way; in fact, I think it is our duty to do so."[33]

Jefferson's Broadcasting Interests

There was a certain consistency in the growth patterns of both Pilot Life and Jefferson Standard:

JOSEPH MCKINLEY BRYAN

JEFFERSON-PILOT'S COMMUNICATIONS arm grew from the mind of Joseph McKinley Bryan, the son of an Ohio bicycle maker and inventor. Bryan was the second son of Bart and Caroline Ebert Bryan. After their divorce, Bryan was sent to live with two aunts in New York.

For a short time he attended a Massachusetts prep school, but when the aunts could no longer afford tuition, he dropped out and joined the Army. The young Bryan came of age during World War I, transporting the sick and wounded and rising to sergeant.

In 1923, at 27, Bryan became the youngest person to be granted membership on the New York Cotton Exchange. He next went to Haiti, where he became a rich man brokering cotton for a New York company.

Back in New York, he met Julian Price's daughter, Kathleen Price, on November 18, 1927. The two married in Greensboro and lived for the next four years in New York City, where two daughters, Kay and Nancy were born. The Bryans later had a son, named after his father. Julian Price, determined to get his daughter back to Greensboro, offered Bryan a job in 1931.

The Bryans moved to Greensboro, and by 1933 he was company secretary and a member of the board of directors of Jefferson Standard. He was promoted to vice president in 1936, first vice president in 1947, and senior vice presi-

dent in 1956. He was chairman of the board of Pilot Life Insurance Company, and he later served as a director of the Jefferson-Pilot Corporation.

Bryan served as a member of the board of Jefferson Standard Life Insurance Company until 1993. He served as senior vice president of Jefferson Standard, chairman of the board of Jefferson Standard Broadcasting Company, and honorary chairman of the board of Pilot Life Insurance Company. Bryan also served on the boards of NCNB (which became Bank of America) and Atlantic and Yadkin Railroad and was one of the original six members of the North Carolina Business Hall of Fame.

Bryan's philanthropy helped create parks, roads, libraries, and civic programs. After Kathleen died of Alzheimer's Disease, he donated more than $10 million to Duke University for Alzheimer's research.

"I had to live down being the son-in-law," he remarked years later about his work at Jefferson Standard. "I don't know that I ever did. It was tough going. I don't say I was abused. . . . I was young. I could take it. I just gave it back to them as fast as they could send it to me."[1]

"He was a very stern, good man," remembered his assistant of twenty-five years, Ann Rambeaut. "He was definitely made of that finer stuff and he had a wit about him."[2]

An advertisement from Jefferson Standard declaring the power of the company's insurance. In the 1930s, Joseph Bryan pushed Jefferson Standard to diversify into communications.

They were both southern insurance companies run by shrewd businessmen and canny investors who were interested in enriching the whole state of North Carolina. This interest often took the form of investments and other activities that had nothing to do with insurance. For example, shortly after World War I, Julian Price had invested $40,000 in the *Greensboro Daily Record*. He later sold his share of the newspaper for $400,000. Although it was a wildly profitable investment, Price's connection to the newspaper was more than idle interest. His daughter, Kathleen Price, was the society editor.

Around this time (1922), WNRC, a tiny, ten-watt radio station, began to broadcast from Greensboro. The station grew slowly until the end of 1926, when Wayne Nelson, the station's owner-operator, reached a sponsorship agreement with the Greensboro Chamber of Commerce. WNRC relocated to the eighth floor of the Jefferson Standard Building; the Chamber broadcast Tuesdays, Thursdays, and Sundays, while Nelson's brand of community-oriented programming and news was broadcast the other four days of the week.[34] Early in 1927, a transmitter was fixed atop the city's only skyscraper, and WNRC went on the air from its new home.

In 1930, WNRC's call letters were changed to WBIG, for "We Believe in Greensboro." Listenership was high among the small number of residents who owned a radio, but ad revenue was insignificant. The station was unable to make the necessary improvements required by the newly created Federal Communications Commission and was about to go off the air.

Despite the dire finances of the local station, some people in the country, including Joseph Bryan at Jefferson Standard, believed the age of radio was coming. In 1933, Franklin Delano Roosevelt gave the first presidential inaugural address over the radio waves, further intriguing Bryan. Then in 1934 an opportunity presented itself. During a bad storm, the transmission tower atop the Jefferson Standard building was destroyed, pushing WBIG into bankruptcy. Bryan moved quickly, convincing Julian Price that the radio waves could be used to build name recognition for Jefferson Standard. After some debate, Price agreed, and in 1934 Jefferson Standard bought WBIG for $10,000.[35] On May 23, 1934, Joseph Bryan was named president of the newly formed North Carolina Broadcasting Company, a subsidiary of Jefferson Standard.[36]

During the years that followed, Bryan saw his intuition borne out. The golden age of radio had indeed arrived, and before too many years passed, Bryan reported to the board of directors that profits from the radio station equaled 100 percent of the original investment.[37]

With the station successfully operating, Bryan next turned to newspapers. With Price's permission, Jefferson Standard made loans to newspapers, such as the *Tulsa Tribune* and *Phoenix Gazette* and to papers in Indianapolis, Denver, San Jose, and Philadelphia.

This new subsidiary, relying on Bryan's keen sense of the emerging media and his relentless travel and promotion, laid the foundation for Jefferson-Pilot Communications, one of the most successful radio and television station owners in the country.

An artesian drinking fountain at Sedgefield. Pilot Life drilled its own wells for the headquarters campus.

CHAPTER THREE
INTO THE MODERN AGE
1940 – 1967

*The elements of humor, gallantry, verve, firmness, tenacity, calculation
and discernment were so mixed in Julian Price as to make him the man,
the business leader and the citizen that he was.*

—*Greensboro Daily News*,
Julian Price's eulogy, 1946

"JOIN UP"
WITH
young
MEN

THE PILOT

W ITH WAR CLOUDS LOOMING, Jefferson Standard and Pilot Life moved from one period of uncertainty to another. Yet there were crucial differences in the texture of the times. In 1940, the Great Depression was already receding into the nation's collective memory. The economic event that had defined a decade was replaced by a booming wartime economy and a great global struggle against fascism. This struggle, which would ultimately claim 40 million lives, began tragically in 1939 and got much worse in the year that followed.

That spring, Nazi troops rolled through northern Europe, taking Denmark in a day and Norway in a few weeks and isolating hundreds of thousands of British troops on the beaches at Dunkirk, forcing them to flee. In June 1940, Hitler rode down the Champs Elysee and accepted France's surrender.

In the Pacific, the situation wasn't much better. Japan exerted its control over Indochina and tightened its grip over China. Finally, in September 1940, Germany, Italy, and Japan signed the Tripartite Pact, forming the Axis powers. In Europe, Britain stood alone, with bombs raining on London every night. In the Pacific, Japan turned its ambitions toward an increasingly isolated Australia and New Zealand. Even before the attack at Pearl Harbor, there seemed very little way for America to avoid the war.

Boom Times in North Carolina

As the nation prepared for war, sales of everything from tanks to life insurance boomed. In 1940, *National Underwriter* ranked Jefferson Standard the 42nd largest insurance company in the country in terms of insurance written. Pilot Life was ranked 58th. These were strong numbers, but Jefferson Standard executives responded by pointing out that too much money was still flowing to the North: $340 million in 1940.[1]

The summer brought continued expansion for Jefferson Standard, which opened offices in Phoenix, Arizona, and Casper, Wyoming, bringing the number of branches to 47 and the number of agents to 1,000. Measured by the amount of insurance written at the end of 1940, Jefferson Standard and Security Life and Trust were overwhelmingly the largest ordinary insurance companies in the state, with $12.3 million and $11.9 million, respectively. Pilot Life wrote $5.7 million that year. Gauged by insurance in force, Pilot Life's $56.4 million was behind only Jefferson Standard's $134 million.[2]

A Pilot Life flyer from 1940, promoting the merit of joining the armed forces on the eve of U.S. participation in World War II. Both companies helped the war effort substantially.

U.S. soldiers march outside the Pilot Life headquarters at Sedgefield. Meanwhile, the U.S. Army Air Corps established administrative offices and officer quarters at the nearby Sedgefield Inn. Jefferson Standard also lent office space to the military for the duration of the war.

Jefferson Standard concentrated on carefully selecting its prospects and agents, direct marketing, and honing its sales training plans.[3] Although the company still didn't advertise much, its marketing focused on increasing sales to working women, widows, teachers, the military, and teenagers. Direct mail promoted new products such as family income insurance and mortgage cancellation insurance.

Still in its building in downtown Greensboro, Jefferson Standard was a complicated operation. In the days when everything was done by hand, a legion of record keepers and file cabinets was required to organize a company as large as Jefferson Standard. In 1940, Seth Macon joined as a file clerk and later recounted how the company kept track of its tens of thousands of policy holders. "In those days, they had a file on every policy, and the key information about that policy was in that file," Macon said. "The main file consisted of the whole 16th floor, and it was a very important job."[4]

Although Pilot Life was still smaller in terms of insurance in force, by 1940 the company's finances were strong enough to finance a major stock buyback. That year, Jefferson Standard authorized the sale of Pilot Life's capital stock, and Pilot Life once again became a private company, ending a decade of ownership by Jefferson Standard. At the time, Pilot Life employed 80 people, and no one doubted that Jefferson Standard and Pilot Life would continue their close relationship.[5]

The War Years

Less than a year after the buyback, the United States was fully involved in World War II. Following the December 1941 attacks on Pearl Harbor, President Franklin Roosevelt asked for, and Congress granted, a U.S. declaration of war on Germany, Italy, and Japan. The war, Roosevelt cautioned Americans, would require great sacrifice in lives, material comfort, and freedoms. The country responded as with a single voice, united behind the president.

Jefferson Standard and Pilot Life would play their parts in the wartime drama while still growing quickly. At the end of 1943, after 36 years of steady growth, Jefferson Standard passed the long anticipated milestone of $500 million of insurance in force.

Both companies also responded to the U.S. military's need for office space and facilities. From 1943 to 1946, U.S. Army Air Corps officers were stationed at Sedgefield Inn, remembered Jim Blackburn, who was manager of the grounds at Pilot Life's Sedgefield complex during World War II. As the armed forces moved in and local men were called up for duty, Blackburn remembered finding himself in charge of the property's private water line.

"I was reading meters, repairing minor leaks, installing new meters, and things of that nature," Blackburn said. "Then I got a notice from my draft board to report to Fort Bragg. I went to the company and said they better get somebody for my job. I'm headed for the navy. The auditor asked for my number and the draft board, and I didn't know anything else until I got a notice that I was deferred. In my own mind, I know the auditor went to the navy and said, 'We're losing the only man that we've got looking after the water and sewer lines, which serve Sedgefield and Pilot Life and parts of Greensboro.' I was never drafted."[6]

Bessie Land, a longtime Pilot Life employee known for her infectious laugh, remembered the tight squeeze as army officers took over more of the headquarters buildings. "Our division was one of the divisions that had to move to make way for the army," Land said. "They took over the east wing and then took over a portion of the main building. We crowded into a smaller office."[7]

Jefferson Standard also donated headquarters and office space in its downtown building. The company regularly sent $25 war bonds to its employees in the armed services.[8] In all, 228 Jefferson Standard employees served in the armed forces. To honor its employees in the service, Jefferson Standard flew a flag with a blue star for each one of them. Yellow stars were added later to honor those killed in the line of duty.

Pilot Life, too, honored its war dead in a 1942 article that appeared in the company newsletter. Next to an announcement that Pilot Life's assets had increased 12 percent, to $27.9 million, the company ran a black-and-white photograph of a young, dark-eyed private who was killed in action. An accompanying article noted that the female students of nearby High Point College were resoundingly in favor of drafting women for work in the armed services and the civil defense industries. Shortly after this article, Pilot Life made headlines by buying an additional $6 million in war bonds, bringing the company's total war bond holdings to nearly $14.7 million. It was the largest purchase of war bonds in the state at that time.

By 1944, victory in the war was in sight as the Axis powers crumbled before Allied armies. In the Pacific, Japanese fleets were defeated at Midway and the Coral Sea. Marines on Guadalcanal won a hard-fought ground battle. In Europe, the D-Day invasion of Normandy opened a new front against the Germans, allowing American troops to roll toward

A wartime insurance calendar. These calendars were popular giveaway items for many decades. Fittingly, healing is a theme for this particular calendar.

Berlin from the west while the Russians pressed from the east. Victory finally arrived in 1945.

During a January 1945 board meeting, while acknowledging its employees who had served or died in the war, Pilot Life announced a $6-a-share dividend and a 5 percent bonus to home office employees.[9] At Jefferson Standard, Julian Price built housing for some of the company's returning veterans to honor their contribution to the war effort.

"He decided to build houses for some of us veterans," remembered Archie Coleman, who joined

The Jefferson Club. Both companies offered their employees private clubs with family activities, day camps, and dining. Many of the children would later join the company.

Jefferson Standard in 1935, then was drafted into the 82nd Airborne Division and fought in Europe. "Most of us were married by then, and he let us rent the houses for about $50 a month. Then the state insurance commissioner decided that he couldn't do that because he wasn't supposed to house his employees. So he had to sell them to us, and the mortgage went up to about $70 a month."[10]

Like Pilot Life's employees at Sedgefield, these Jefferson Standard employees quickly developed a tight bond that encompassed work, family, and recreation. "This group of people was so close to the Jefferson Club, all the kids would walk through the woods to the club and go to the lake to swim," Coleman said. "It was kind of family. At Christmastime, we'd go hunting on Jefferson Standard property, then go to the club and have all our kids over for hot chocolate and lunch. It was nice."[11]

Randy Macon grew up in one of the Jefferson Road houses. The son of Seth Macon, Randy would join Pilot Life in 1975. "As a child, I spent a lot of time at the club," he remembered. "I went to day

camp there, so for the entire month of July, I was at a day camp filled with kids from Jefferson Standard families. At that time, every parent and every kid had a tie to Jefferson Standard."[12]

While the veterans were still settling into the new houses on Jefferson Road, Julian Price penned an optimistic message to shareholders. He wrote, "To you, at this opening of a new year, Jefferson Standard brings a message of confidence that life insurance will continue to guarantee the economic security of the individual in true American fashion."[13]

After the War: Julian Price Steps Down

These uplifting words, written on his 34th anniversary with the company, would appear in Julian Price's last letter to shareholders. He had led the company through the Depression and World War II. Under his tutelage, Jefferson Standard had become one of the largest life insurance companies in America, with more than half a billion dollars of insurance in force.

"He had what they call the golden touch," remembered Bill Seawell Jr., who joined the company in 1940 and later rose to vice president of marketing services. "He not only ran the sales department, but he also handled all the big investments the company made. Everything he did turned out good."[14]

The Agency Department was headed by M. A. "Jack" White, who held the position from 1943 to 1947. Joe Bryan, Price's son-in-law and president of the communications division, was elected to the board of directors and executive committee in 1942. As always, Julian Price was modest about the accomplishment of his company. As he announced that the company was passing $500

million of insurance in force, he told employees, "To have seen this day is a privilege greater than any I have ever enjoyed."[15]

Jack Scism, of the *Greensboro News & Record*, summed up Price as his career came to a close: "He is confident, cantankerous, dynamic, driven, opinionated, outgoing. Even his enemies, and he accumulated a few over the years, conceded his genius. He had no formal education in finance, but he had willpower."[16]

Thus when Julian Price announced his retirement in late 1944, newspapers, magazines, and radio programs across the state remarked on the event. As he stepped down, he put his plan for succession into place. He was named chairman of Jefferson Standard, and according to his wishes,

Julian and Ralph Price in 1946. When Julian Price stepped down from the helm of Jefferson Standard in 1945, he had arranged for his son to take the reins.

his son, Ralph C. Price, was voted president. The younger Price was a graduate of the University of North Carolina and Harvard Business School and had worked his way up from agent to head of the Agency Department in 1938.

Sadly, Julian Price would not enjoy his retirement years. In 1944, the same year he stepped down, his wife of 46 years, Ethel Clay Price, died. Only two years later, after placing flowers on the grave of his wife, Julian Price himself was killed in a car crash while heading to his mountain property outside of Blowing Rock, North Carolina. He was going up to check on the progress of a dam he was building, hoping to create a hotel and small lake for fishing and swimming on several thousand private acres.

Price's death provoked a statewide outpouring of emotion. More than 2,000 mourners attended his funeral at the First Presbyterian Church.[17] Tributes came in for weeks, both from the statewide press and from inside the company. "He was challenging," remembered Joe Webster Jr., a Jefferson Standard agent since 1939 and a lifetime member of the Million Dollar Round Table. "Julian Price was also generous. I remember one story about him. He was stopped by a man who told him he wanted some money to buy shoes. Mr. Price said, 'You come on up here with me.' He took him up to his office and took his own shoes off and said, 'See if those will fit you.' When they did, he said, 'You just go ahead and take those.' The man said. 'What are you going to do?' Mr. Price said, 'I've got another pair at home.'"[18]

This story became such a part of Julian Price's legacy that the *Spartanburg Herald*, in South Carolina, recounted it after Price died. The *North Carolina Catholic* newspaper also remarked that it had lost one of its best friends. The summer before his death, Price had given $400,000 for the construction of a Catholic church in Greensboro as a memorial to his wife, who had been a Catholic.

"Julian Price never ran away from a fight, but whatever position he took, whatever conviction he held, there was no hesitation in stating it, no swerving from the course of deliberate and direct action," eulogized the *Greensboro Daily News*. "The elements of humor, gallantry, verve, firmness, tenacity, calculation and discernment were so mixed in Julian Price as to make him the man, the business leader and the citizen that he was."[19]

Price was also a member or trustee of a number of political, state, educational, humanitarian, and business institutions. He was a 33rd degree Mason, a commander of the Knights Templar, a member emeritus of the Imperial Council of Ancient Arabic Order of Nobles of the Mystic Shrine (Shriners), and a member of Rotary and other civic clubs. Among his philanthropic contributions was the establishment of a foundation to promote education and assist the University of North Carolina at Chapel Hill with development efforts.

Julian Price Memorial Park is enjoyed by millions of locals and tourists who boat, fish, picnic, camp, and ride horses in the park and along its miles of gentle mountain trails. At 4,300 acres, it is the largest recreational facility on the Blue Ridge Parkway. After his death, the company, along with Price's children, Ralph Price and Kathleen Price Bryan, gave the land to the U.S. Department of the Interior for the Parkway.

A Reunion

Before he died, Julian Price negotiated one last deal for his company. The deal was one of the largest financial transactions in Greensboro's history, establishing one of the largest multiple-line insurance companies in the country. On July 1, 1945, Pilot Life and Gate City Life Insurance were purchased and merged by Jefferson Standard in a single, complex transaction.

Jefferson Standard offered $600 per share for each of the 10,000 outstanding shares of Pilot Life.[20] At the time, the shares had a per share value of $100, making the deal too good to pass up. In fact, before the announcement, most of the large stockholders had been consulted and had agreed to back the purchase.

Gate City, which was controlled by Jefferson Standard, became involved in the deal early on. In 1944, the last year it operated as Gate City, the company boasted more than $80 million of insurance

Opposite: Julian Price and his wife, Ethel Clay Price. Sadly, Ethel died the same year Julian retired, and he was killed in a car accident two years later. Julian Price's legacy lived on in North Carolina, however, even beyond the company he built.

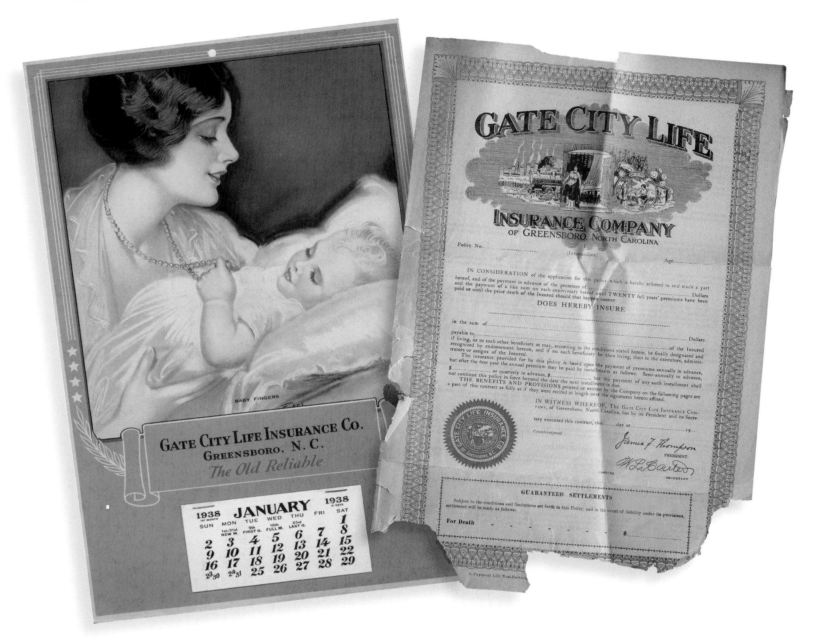

A calendar, left, and policy, right, from Gate City Life Insurance Company. In 1945, Gate City and Pilot Life were merged and acquired by Jefferson Standard.

in force. In 1945, months before the final transaction, Gate City was merged into Pilot Life. Unlike its larger brethren, Gate City operated completely within the state boundaries of North Carolina, and it boasted one of the largest group insurance divisions in the South.[21]

The division was in fact the jewel in Gate City's crown. Group insurance was still new to America, and in some places it even seemed a little illegal—although it wasn't. Joe Freeman Sr., who headed up group insurance at Gate City and later at Pilot Life, recalled rounding up 100 people at a time and snapping a picture for an insurance policy.

As Gate City and Pilot Life merged, Gate City disappeared into Pilot Life, which received new leadership. Emry Green, the president of Pilot Life, stepped aside in 1946 in favor of O. F. Stafford, the 42-year-old president of Gate City.

Pilot Life and Jefferson Standard continued to operate as separate entities, maintaining their tradition of separate cultures and friendly competition. The combined company offered ordinary life insurance through Jefferson Standard and Pilot Life, in addition to maintaining Gate City's robust group insurance and Pilot Life's industrial operations.

Growth in the Forties

The merger took place at a remarkable time in American history. By the end of 1945, World War II was over, leaving both tragedy and opportunity in its wake. Much of Europe was destroyed, and the old social orders that had governed the continent were gone. Similarly, Asia lay in ruins, and much of the world's industrial infrastructure was damaged or destroyed.

Into this vacuum of power and wealth stepped an eager United States. Alone among industrialized nations, the United States had suffered no damage to its major industries. Primed by wartime production, the American industrial plant was the envy of the world. With astonishing rapidity, American industry shifted from military production to consumer production, and new goods flooded a hungry marketplace. Televisions soon proliferated, and technologies like wristwatches and washing machines weren't far behind. These goods were eagerly purchased by young families setting up house in another new phenomenon: the suburbs.

Jefferson Standard and Pilot Life responded. For its part, Jefferson Standard was one of the country's first insurance companies to recognize the power of radio advertising. In the 1940s, Jefferson Standard hired NBC to prepare radio announcements that could be personalized by each agent. The 45-second spot allowed a 15-second tie-in. The home office paid half the cost for each spot to air.

The most potent advertising, however, came from the government and the millions of veterans. Until the 1940s, farmers were the country's largest occupational group, and insurance companies had traditionally focused on reaching them. Agents made an effective case that insurance was necessary to protect the family and the farm in the event of a disaster.

In the 1940s, however, the very idea of life insurance received a major boost as soldiers returned from the war. The military made a practice of offering life insurance to soldiers. For many soldiers, this was their first experience with life insurance, and they had grown used to the peace of mind it afforded. Second, a new program called Social Security was in the offing. This ambitious government program was a forced savings program to help support the elderly in retirement. During the legislative debate, a National Service Life Insurance policy was added as a veteran's benefit to Social Security.

This formal announcement heralded the merger of Pilot Life and Gate City. The merger doubled the size of Pilot Life's group division, making Pilot Life one of the largest group insurers in the South.

Jefferson Standard responded by developing insurance products that complemented Social Security.

Driven by a booming population with increasing financial savvy, Jefferson Standard and Pilot Life entered a period of rapid growth. In 1946, 1,200 Jefferson Standard field representatives wrote more than $114 million in new business.[22] The company was active in 28 states, the District of Columbia, and Puerto Rico. The next year began even better: In the first six months of 1947, Jefferson Standard agents wrote $60 million of insurance, breaking the previous record. By year end, the company had more than $100 million of new business.[23]

In 1948, only 28 companies in the United States had more ordinary life insurance in force than Jefferson Standard did. Only 31 had more assets.

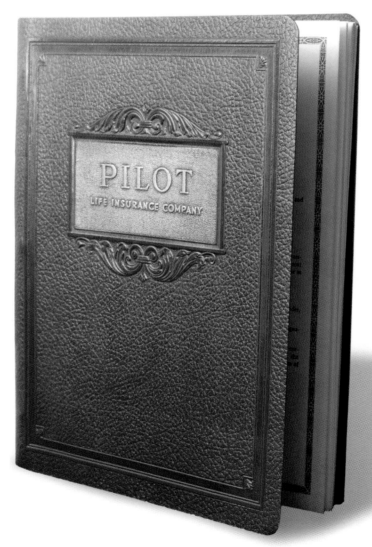

The company placed 22nd in amount of capital and surplus funds. There were 71 branch offices and district offices in 30 states, the District of Columbia, and Puerto Rico.[24] More than 300,000 individual policies were in force, amounting to more than $800 million. More than 500 employees worked out of the home office and seven North Carolina branches, drawing an annual payroll of $1.27 million.

Pilot Life, too, fared well during these years. In 1948, the company boasted $448 million of insurance in force and record assets of $64.8 million.[25] Much of the company's growth was due to its Industrial Weekly Premium Department. By 1945, Pilot Life had $74 million of insurance in force through its industrial division alone. With the Gate City merger, Pilot Life added $135 million of group insurance, establishing Pilot Life as one of the major group insurance companies in the country.[26]

After the Gate City merger, Pilot Life continued to innovate with its group product line. In 1948, Pilot Life began to offer scholastic accident insurance for school children, offering $10,000 of annual coverage for a dollar a year. The idea took off with everyone from grade school principals to high school football coaches. By the close of 1951, the Group Department was insuring 470,000 school children and teachers; within four years Pilot Life was selling $1 million of scholastic accident insurance annually. Joe Freeman Sr. was a driving force behind group scholastic insurance.

"For a dollar a year, everyone bought it," Joe Freeman Jr., son of Joe Freeman Sr., remembered. "Even if it was a money-losing deal, Dad's theory was, 'You might not be making money on it, but how else can you advertise from the first day? The kid is in first grade and he's got a Pilot Life card in his pocket. He'll carry that all the way through to college!'"[27]

As the 1940s finished, Jefferson Standard and Pilot Life sat astride a national wave of prosperity and growth. They had increased both their insurance in force and the size of their investment portfolios. By 1947, Jefferson Standard had made more

A Pilot Life group insurance contract. Joe Freeman Sr. remembered assembling groups of 100 people in the early days and snapping their picture to qualify them for coverage.

Even during the globalization of the 1950s, Jefferson Standard maintained an unusual presence in the Spanish-speaking Caribbean. This postcard showed the company's Puerto Rico office, and the policy is written in Spanish.

than 2,000 loans at 5.1 percent interest. *Best's Life Insurance Report*, which published an annual cost analysis based on the actual 20-year history of insurance companies, placed Jefferson Standard near the top of the list. For a number of years, Jefferson Standard's whole life policies and 20-year endowment policies provided more actual benefits for less cost during a 20-year period than any other company's.[28]

By 1948, Jefferson Standard boasted $221 million in assets against $194 million in liabilities and insurance in force of $820 million. The company was in an excellent position to finish out the year. In the 1949 annual report, Jefferson Standard reported that it had earned a higher rate of interest on investments than any other major life insurance company for 13 consecutive years. Net return that year was 4.3 percent, which allowed the company

HOWARD HOLDERNESS

HOLDERNESS WAS BORN IN 1902. HIS father, George A. Holderness, had helped organize Jefferson Standard and served as vice president and chairman of the Jefferson Standard board of directors. George Holderness was an executive of the old school, when executives prided themselves on knowing the names of employees, their wives, and even their children. He was remembered as "the friend of every Jefferson Standard official and employee." This kind of description appears again and again throughout the written and oral histories of both Jefferson Standard and Pilot Life.

Howard was sent to Augusta Military Academy in Georgia and then to the University of North Carolina at Chapel Hill, where his grades earned him a place in the nation's highest academic fraternity, Phi Beta Kappa.

At about the time he was earning a Phi Beta Kappa key, however, he was acquiring something equally important, his nickname, "Chick." Holderness played on a Tarboro baseball team, one of the hundreds of baseball teams in industrial leagues. Holderness was the catcher, the player who sees the whole field, the one who must be alert to all possibilities of which the other team might take advantage. One of his teammates dubbed him "Chick," the moniker of a catcher then playing for the old St. Louis Browns. The name stuck, and in May 1950, when Holderness was

elected president of Jefferson Standard, it was still there.

"When I introduce him to a new agent," a colleague said at the time, "I wouldn't think of introducing him as anything but 'Chick.'"[1]

One summer during his college years, Holderness worked in Jefferson Standard's actuarial department in Greensboro. After he graduated in 1923, he went on to the Harvard University School of Business Administration. He earned a master's degree in 1925 and returned to Jefferson Standard's mortgage loan department.

Holderness worked in the department for seven years. The Great Depression provided rigorous training ground for someone who would one day control the company. Holderness was made manager of the mortgage loan department in 1931.

In 1932, the year of Franklin D. Roosevelt's election as U.S. president, Holderness was named vice president and treasurer; at the same time, he was elected to the board of directors. In April 1936, he married Adelaide Fortune, the daughter of a Greensboro physician. They had five children, two sons and three daughters.[2]

In 1945, after Ralph Price was elevated to the leadership position, Holderness left the company to start his own investment business. He returned five years later as president.

to continue its long history of paying 4 percent interest on funds deposited by policy holders and beneficiaries. At the end of 1949, Jefferson Standard operated 72 branch offices in 30 states, the District of Columbia, and Puerto Rico.

This enviable record of growth, scope, and successful investments led Jefferson Standard to announce a bold goal in 1949: $1 billion of insurance in force. A new banner was unveiled that proclaimed the company "Billion Bound."

A New Decade

These were good years for optimism. By 1950, American families were busily producing what later became known as the "baby boom," referring to the millions of children born to returning veterans. At the same time, the country entered a period of prosperity that would not be matched until the 1990s. American companies circled the globe, rebuilding shattered economies and selling goods. Consumer technology leaped forward, making affordable everything from household appliances to consumer electronics.

Jefferson Standard and Pilot Life were perfectly positioned to ride this wave of prosperity. Between 1950 and 1970, the population of America grew from 150 million to 203 million. Much of this population growth occurred in the southern "Sun Belt" states, where northerners moved to avoid winter and industry moved to avoid taxes. These states, traditionally the poorest in the country, were becoming more affluent and more populous. Between 1950 and 1955, national income grew from $241.1 billion to $331 billion. By 1959, national income would approach $415 billion.[29] Much of this growth would be concentrated in the South.

In 1950, Jefferson Standard hit $900 million of insurance in force, just shy of its $1 billion goal. It seemed assured that the next year would bring realization of its goal. Yet once again, changes were afoot in the executive suite. By 1950, Ralph Price had been president of Jefferson Standard for only four years, but the board of directors was looking for new leadership. "Ralph was not the kind of leader that his father was," recalled Seth Macon. "Ralph, after his father's death, had difficulty in his decision making."[30]

To replace Price, the board called on Howard Holderness, bringing him back from a self-imposed exile. A longtime veteran of Jefferson Standard, Holderness had left the company in 1945 when it became clear that Julian Price was grooming his son to take over. It was a difficult decision for Holderness, who had spent his entire adult career with Jefferson Standard. He had roomed with Ralph Price during college and was the son of George A. Holderness, one of the founders of Jefferson Standard. After he left, he formed an investment company, Holderness & Company Investments, with his brother.[31] The new company's offices were located a few blocks down the street from Jefferson Standard.

In 1950, the board approached Holderness and asked him to return to Jefferson Standard as president. He accepted the offer, but the transition would not be smooth. Ralph Price had no immediate plans to step aside, and he had considerable clout from his family's stock and some of the board members.

The situation was further complicated by Joseph M. Bryan, Ralph's brother-in-law. Bryan was also a board member and senior executive. When he saw a potential opening, he announced his own candidacy for president and began to lobby for board support.

"Ralph Price and Joe Bryan got crossed up," remembered Macon. "They had to keep their stock together in order to control. When they got crossed up, Joe said, 'I'm not going to vote with you, and then the Prices no longer will have control.' Joe thought he was going to become president. He organized a series of employee meetings—I attended them—in which he was trying to sell the idea that he was going to be a good leader when he became president. Well, everybody, or a lot of people, thought he was going to become president."[32]

At that point, things took an unexpected turn when a board member named Jack Lindley stepped in. Lindley was the son of John Van Lindley, a founder of the Greensboro Life Insurance Company, and through his family he controlled voting rights on a significant portion of Jefferson Standard stock.[33] Lindley supported Holderness for the presidency and presented him to the board as his choice. The rest of the board members fell in line and approved Howard Holderness as the company's new president.

But the situation was not so easily resolved. Although Holderness had been voted president by the company, Jefferson Standard's bylaws dictated that the president of the company also be president of the board, a position he did not hold. Ralph Price was president of the board. Nevertheless, Holderness moved into his new office, and "for about two or three weeks, Ralph was the president, while directly across the hall was his former college roommate, Holderness, who also was president."[34]

The situation was finally resolved when Ralph Price relinquished the presidency and resigned. The way was clear for Howard Holderness to imprint Jefferson Standard with his own brand of leadership.

The Pilot Evolves

While the leadership situation settled down at Jefferson Standard, Pilot Life continued to forge ahead under O. F. Stafford. Five years into office, Stafford had made a favorable impression throughout the company. He was a local boy who had risen through the company by hard work and intelligence. He was more humble than Holderness, in both background and bearing, and he wore his roots openly. He had attended Greensboro public schools and a nearby Quaker college named Guilford College, then began his career walking throughout the countryside collecting weekly premiums. In his early days, Stafford covered eight to ten miles a day on foot.[35]

When he was named president, Stafford carried his common touch with him. He ate in the employees' cafeteria and was very accessible and charming to employees. Nancy Elkins, who joined during Stafford's presidency, remembered a congenial atmosphere, deeply imprinted with Stafford's personality.

"I was 20 years old," Elkins said. "The company had employee dances at the club, so I went to a dance within a few weeks after I first started to work, and there was Mr. Stafford. I thought, 'Oh my, there's the president of the company.' He went around and he talked to everybody. I was really impressed with this."[36]

His temperament was a perfect fit with Pilot Life. Many employees fondly remembered the company trips up to Pilot Mountain or the car pooling and bus service to get to Sedgefield. "On the buses, we'd carry on, you know, laughing, talking with the

O. F. STAFFORD

OGBURN FLETCHER "O. F." STAFFORD became president of Pilot Life in 1946 at the age of 42.

Stafford had studied two years at Guilford College before going to work for Gate City, walking the rolling countryside collecting rural debit insurance, often covering eight to ten miles a day. His rise through the company was immediate. In 1926 he was elected secretary and treasurer of Gate City and was named president in 1938. Upon the merger with Pilot in 1945, he was named assistant to the chairman of the board, then president of Pilot Life at the January 1946 board of directors meeting. He was elected chairman of the board and chief executive officer of Pilot in July 1968 and held that position until he died in November of that same year.

Stafford was the sort of man who, even when he held the position of president of Pilot Life, shunned the executive dining rooms and instead carried his own tray in the company cafeteria. He made a point of being close to Pilot employees. "I feel the people here work with me, not for me," he once said. He maintained an open-door policy, even when Pilot's home-office staff swelled to 600. "There were so few employees when I first came to work that it seemed like a family," he said. "I've tried to keep it that way."

different riders," remembered Bessie Land, who joined Pilot Life in 1928 and retired in 1975. "We were just one big family."[37]

Stafford, who carried his crooked pipe everywhere he went, was described as "an involved man.

Opposite: O. F. Stafford with his trademark "crooked pipe." Stafford came to the company from Gate City Life, where his insurance career began with him walking country roads to collect weekly premiums.

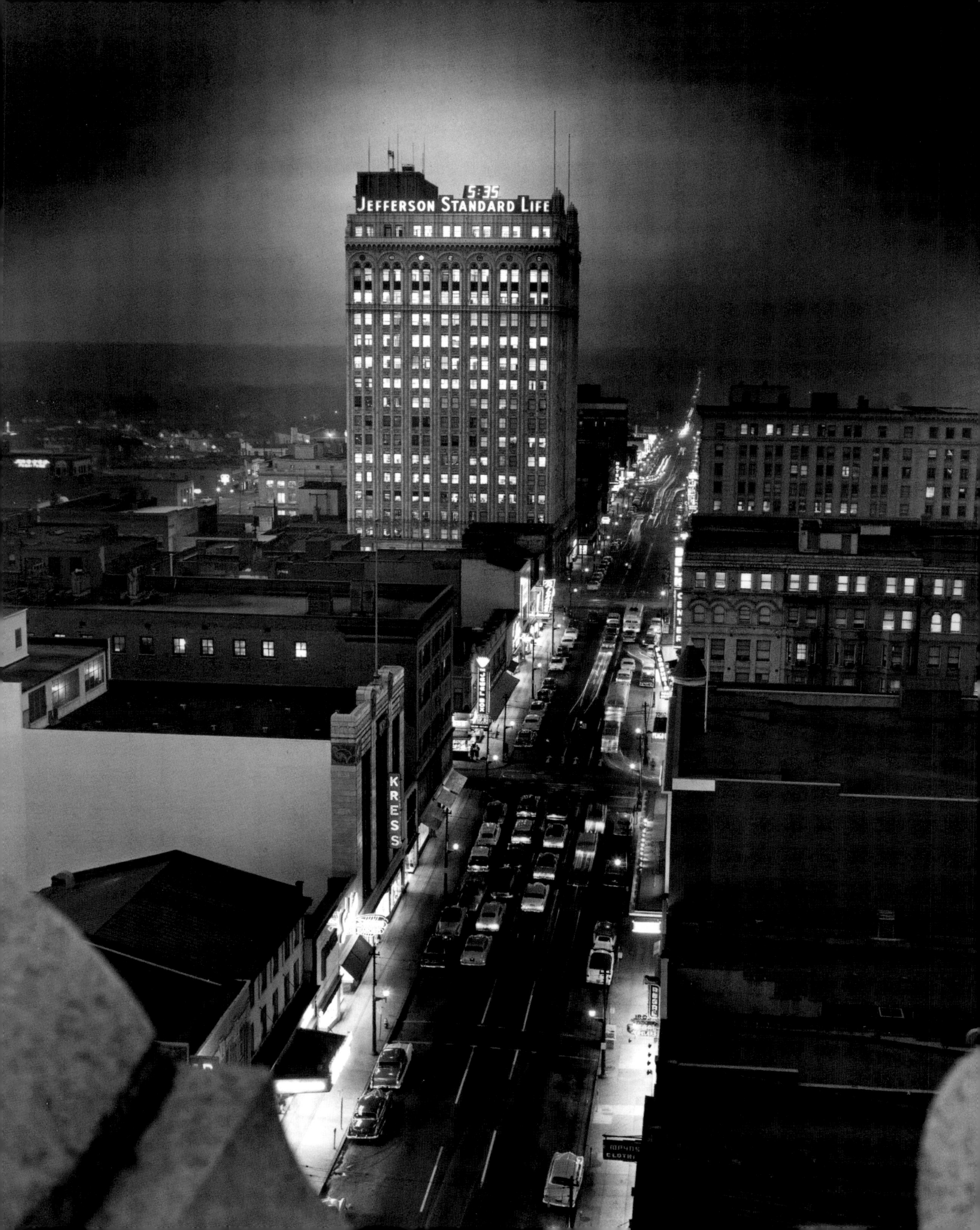
5:35
JEFFERSON STANDARD LIFE
KRESS

Scholarly in appearance, quiet in manner, soft and Southern in speech, he genuinely liked people, and he gave to them. He gave his time, his thoughts, and his support."[38]

He was nevertheless a fierce competitor, and it was during his tenure that Pilot Life began to overtake Jefferson Standard in insurance in force. On January 23, 1951, Stafford presented the sales figures for 1950, saying, "Gaining more than $50 million life insurance in force for 1950, Pilot Life Insurance Company passed the half-billion-dollar mark early in the year and went on to establish an all-time high for the company of $533,844,811 at year's end. The gain in insurance in force was 52 percent greater than the gain in the previous year."[39] He went on to note that 1950 was the fifth consecutive year in which Pilot Life wrote at least $100 million in new policies.[40]

Behind this growth was Pilot Life's increasing reliance on the youth market. In the early 1950s, the company sought permission to go into schools and offer a prize to every child who filled out a report, furnished by the agency, as to safety conditions at home. The reports documented common hazards and promoted fire and chemical safety.

One example was the popular new cleaning mops that were soaked in cedar oil. If not stored in properly ventilated places, the mops were "liable to spontaneous combustion and have caused a number of dwelling-house fires." Children were instructed to notice and report on such potential dangers. In response, the agencies gave "absolutely free to each school child, of school age . . . a good book bag upon the delivery of this paper to us with all questions properly answered." With every book bag, of course, came a pitch to the parents about buying fire insurance.

Pilot Life's innovations were recognized. "Pilot Life pioneered scholastic accident insurance after Dr. Elmer Garinger, superintendent of schools of Charlotte, asked for some sort of coverage that would protect youngsters from the time they left home for school until they returned to their homes in the afternoon," a North Carolina magazine explained. "Pilot Life began to write scholastic accident policies—at $1 per student—in 1948. By 1952 Pilot Life was selling $1 million worth of scholastic accident insurance a year. It leads the South in this area and may rank number one in the nation."[41]

The company expanded its product line in other directions as well. In 1950, Pilot Life organized an Accident and Health Department to write individual hospitalization policies. (The company's original accident and health department had been sold in the 1930s.) That same year, plans were announced for a five-story addition to the Sedgefield headquarters.

The local investment in Sedgefield represented only a fraction of what Pilot Life poured into the North Carolina economy through its investment portfolio. In December 1953, *The State* magazine reported on Pilot Life's contributions to the state:

"Today, something like $24 million flows into Pilot Life's offices at Sedgefield every year. Roughly $20 million comes to the company in the form of premiums on insurance policies. The rest represents the income earned by company investments. This money—about $2 million a month—is plowed into the economy of the South.

"Pilot Life is investing some $40,000 every working day of the year into the tremendous home-building program that has been underway in the South since 1945. It is customary to marvel at the spanking new coat of paint the South has received since 1945. Marvel also at the financial power that has made this brush-work possible."[42]

The company continued on its upward trajectory throughout the rest of the decade. In February 1955, Stafford reported, "The year 1954 will stand out in Pilot Life's history as the year in which we passed the $100 million mark in total payments to policy holders and to their beneficiaries since the founding of the Company, and the year in which we experienced the largest growth during our 51 years of service. Within the ten-year period just ending our total volume of life insurance has tripled."[43]

In 1959, after 10 years of blistering growth, Stafford reported that the company could look back with satisfaction on an excellent decade while preparing for the future. Inflation, he said, was "a creeping influence that is bad for each of us and is in need of being checked. We should all exert every

Opposite: The Jefferson Standard building in downtown Greensboro in the 1960s. The building still dominated the skyline, decades after its construction.

In 1951, Jefferson Standard achieved $1 billion of insurance in force. It was a major milestone, making Jefferson Standard one of the largest southern insurance companies.

effort to curb this menace and stabilize our economy for the benefit of all our people." In the wake of the U.S. surgeon general's report on the hazards of smoking and its effect on life span, Stafford remarked, "Noteworthy, too, are the continuing efforts by the entire insurance industry to further health education, to make America a healthier and safer place to live."[44]

Pilot Life ended the decade with 1,800 employees and agents, who had produced nearly $243 million in total sales during 1959, more than twice the level at the beginning of the decade. Insurance in force peaked at $1.6 billion. Assets stood at $194.8 million, a gain of nearly $15 million during the year. Income for the year was $55.5 million, and the company ended the decade with $119 in assets for each $100 in liabilities. That year, a second addition was under construction at Sedgefield.

Jefferson Standard

In 1951, with much fanfare, Jefferson Standard crossed the threshold of $1 billion of insurance in force. To celebrate, the company had a party with Gene Autry in attendance. Four years later, Pilot Life broke the same barrier. In 1960, Jefferson Standard would hit $2 billion of insurance in force. It would take Pilot Life only until 1962.

Jefferson Standard's growth in this period is at least partially owed to its successful investment department, which was run by George Cavanaugh, chief financial officer. The investment operation had two arms: a securities department and a mortgage department. While most insurance companies had securities departments, the mortgage department was a particular strength at Jefferson Standard.

Between 1944 and 1950, home ownership in America increased tenfold, to 1.7 million single-family homes. These new homes tended to congregate in the new subdivisions, which in turn provoked a burst of commercial real estate development. According to Roger Soles, an accountant who joined Jefferson Standard's investment operation on the

1951
the year of the Billion

A JEFFERSON STANDARD POLICY *is a* DECLARATION OF INDEPENDENCE *for* THE FAMILY

JEFFERSON STANDARD

securities side in 1947 and later became president of the company, Jefferson Standard focused on commercial mortgage lending. "Not many companies made mortgage loans to the extent that we did," Soles remembered.[45]

Jefferson Standard relied on life insurance agents to sell mortgages. In Holderness' first full year as president, Jefferson Standard "increased its mortgage loan investments very materially," according to the 1951 annual report. "Volume of new mortgage loans made in 1951 was the largest in history. Total first mortgage holdings now amount to $137 million, compared to $120 million at the close of 1950."[46]

While the mortgage department was writing loans, the securities department was thriving under Soles' leadership. Run like a traditional investment operation, the securities department invested in stocks, corporate bonds, and private placement loans. In the 1950s, Jack Warmath joined the securities department as an analyst. He would rise to executive vice president.

"We were one of the early companies to have a stock portfolio," Warmath remembered. "Back in the late 1940s and early 1950s, we were buying common stocks. Most of our investments, however, were private placements and corporate bonds."[47]

Wherever it put its investments, Jefferson Standard was a careful company. During private placements, for instance, analysts from Jefferson Standard always made a trip to the headquarters to get audit reports and meet the management. "That was the most important thing," Warmath remembered. "To visit with the management and do our own credit work."[48]

Investment activity, of course, was only one part of Jefferson Standard's success during the baby boom years. Selling protection for the security and well-being of the families moving into those new homes was the other side. "Eighty-three million Americans now own some form of life insurance protection," declared Jefferson Standard in 1951. "Through war and peace, through depressions and periods of prosperity, the American people have learned that they can rely on life insurance for security. As our nation grows in population and as our standard of living improves, an even greater responsibility for the well-being and protection of our families will fall upon the life insurance industry."[49]

Nevertheless, Jefferson Standard maintained that the country was grossly underinsured. The company pointed to figures compiled by the Federal Reserve Board that showed that even in the highest income bracket, 6 percent of Americans had no life insurance at all and 26 percent put less than $200 a year into life insurance.[50]

Records continued to be set throughout the decade, and the company grew in sophistication and prestige. In 1950, Jefferson Standard had assets of $265.3 million, about three quarters of which were first mortgages. During 1951, assets grew to $296.1 million. With reserves of $36 million, the company had $113.84 in assets for every $100 of liabilities. In addition, Jefferson Standard boasted more than 325,000 policy holders. In 1955, total sales rose to $209 million, a 26 percent increase over 1954 and the largest increase in insurance in force in the company's history: $127 million.

"We closed the year with $1,141,444,047 insurance in force," said the 1955 annual report, "which is almost 2 times the amount in force ten years ago. A large percentage of our sales in 1955 was for the purpose of solving problems related to business and tax situations." Assets were at $429.7 million.[51]

MISS MARY

WHILE PEOPLE LIKE JULIAN PRICE were crucial to building the company, many of Jefferson Standard's beloved figures could be found on lower rungs of the corporate ladder. Probably the most famous among these was Miss Mary Taylor.

Miss Mary, as she was known, worked in the Jefferson Standard building in downtown Greensboro for decades. She started with the company in 1905 and became Julian Price's secretary in 1912. That year, she also took over the company's newsletter, *The Jeffersonian.*

Even after losing her sight in a chemical burn from misprescribed eye drops, Miss Mary continued to produce the company newsletter and stay in touch with the field agents. It was not uncommon for "Miss Mary" to write 25 letters a day on behalf of the company; several decades later, when she was afforded a secretary, she continued her habit of personally writing letters.

"Everybody who was an agent really thought so much of her," remembered Bill Seawell Jr., who worked at Jefferson Standard from 1940 to 1986. "She not only put out the magazine; she wrote birthday letters and kept in touch with the field. She was quite a lady."[1]

Miss Mary was a venerable Jefferson Standard icon, known to all the field agents. Here she is announcing that the $1 billion milestone had been achieved.

A group of Jefferson Standard home office people assemble a replica of the Jefferson Standard building in honor of the $1 billion achievement. Among the staff members pictured are Seth Macon, standing fourth from left, Miss Mary Taylor, seated, and Karl Ljung, also seated.

That year, Holderness decided to create an in-house legal department. Until this time, Jefferson Standard's legal needs were handled by a local Greensboro law firm. The board of directors soon located B. Edward Hudgins, an attorney in Greensboro. He was named Jefferson Standard's first general counsel, in addition to vice president and a director of the company. Shortly afterward, Hudgins approached several colleagues and asked them to join Jefferson Standard's legal department. Among them was Robert H. Koonts, who joined in 1957 and would eventually rise to general counsel. "Mr. Hudgins was a marvelous person, a Rhodes scholar and a gentleman," Koonts remembered of his mentor.[52]

By 1959, the average new policy size was $6,860. Sales approached $235 million, and insurance in force at year's end had reached $1.9 billion. Assets were in excess of $585.5 million.[53]

The success that Pilot Life and Jefferson Standard achieved under the leadership of O. F. Stafford and Howard Holderness resulted not from pressure and tension but from strong leadership. Stafford, for his part, was still known as the man who had once walked miles along North Carolina's dirt roads to collect premiums and had a reputation for a "keen wit" and "everlasting cordiality." As for Holderness, his reputation for affability remained unblemished. "I don't think I have ever heard him give a direct order," an employee would later say of him. "It usually was in the form of a suggestion. But when he did it, he didn't leave you feeling as though you didn't have any sense."[54]

A New Decade Begins

The 1960s would be remembered as the decade when Pilot Life actually passed Jefferson Standard. Their competition, however, remained almost genial. Whichever side "won," the companies' bottom lines were the real victors, and their employees developed a unique culture of friendly competition. "PILOT DEFEATS JEFFERSON," crowed the headline in a 1966 issue of the magazine *Life with Pilot*, "IN Bowling."[55]

That was about as serious as the hostility got; each company stuck to what it did best—agency people setting records for sales, home office people multiplying conservative investments—in a time of continuing expansion. During the 1960s, the population of the United States grew from 180.7 million to 203.2 million, and in the South and West, the prime areas for both Pilot Life and Jefferson Standard agents, population grew disproportionately. Between 1960 and 1970, nearly half of the population increase in the United States occurred in the 22 states of the Sun Belt and the West Coast.[56]

Pilot Life home office personnel and agents gather to celebrate the company's 50th anniversary in 1953. O. F. Stafford is seated in the second row, seventh from right.

Jefferson Standard executives gather on the rooftop to celebrate the company's 50th anniversary in 1957. Roger Soles is sixth from right.

This surge in population would be accompanied by a corresponding surge in financial sophistication and well-being. The 1960s were an interesting decade, rife with contradiction. On the one hand, the economy was growing quickly and household finances were sound. It was a decade of prosperity and employment.

On the other hand, the 1960s would mostly be remembered for the strong passions, fundamental social change and tragedy of those turbulent years. In 1960, American life continued to move to rhythms of the 1940s and 1950s, yet the children of the baby boom were coming of age, and they were developing a new social consciousness attuned to such movements as women's liberation and Civil Rights. These, coupled with the assassination of President John F. Kennedy and the escalating war in Vietnam, led many Americans to conclude that an old era was ending and a new one beginning.

In this new era, across the nation, total life insurance in force surged from $586 billion in 1960 to $1.4 trillion in 1970; the total number of policies grew from 282 million to 355 million. Coverage per family doubled, from $10,200 to $20,700; coverage per insured family doubled, from

$12,700 to $24,400; and the average size of an ordinary life policy grew from $3,360 to $6,110. In 1968, national income reached $714.4 billion, nearly $300 billion more than it had been at the beginning of the decade.[57]

By mid-decade, Pilot Life surpassed Jefferson Standard in insurance in force. Pilot Life hit $3 billion in 1965, followed by Jefferson Standard in 1967. By the end of the decade, Pilot Life would achieve $5 billion of insurance in force, something that Jefferson Standard would not achieve until 1976.

Pilot Life's success was due to several factors, including its decade-old focus on children and young adults. Operating through the schools, giving out free tote bags, Pilot Life had truly become a household name throughout North Carolina, one that conveyed trust, financial security, and protection. In the 1960s, Pilot Life would once again follow the Baby Boomers, moving with them as they graduated from primary and secondary schools and went to college.

This focus on children and young adults fit perfectly with the emergence of television. By the 1960s, television was truly a mass medium. Although there were only a few channels, American families had begun to see its entertainment potential, much of which had to do with sports—already a craze in North Carolina and much of the South.

As early as the 1950s, Pilot Life had begun advertising in televised sporting events around North Carolina. Eager to tap into the emerging power of the new medium, it bought spots in almost any sporting event, even Little League baseball games. Then in 1957, a bigger opportunity opened up, remembered Dick Andrews, named vice president of public relations in 1965.

"The University of North Carolina, one of the leading schools in the Atlantic Coast Conference, had just finished a season of 32 wins and no losses," Andrews later explained. "The team went to play Kansas and Wilt Chamberlain at Kansas State University. North Carolina won the national championship. At the time, we had been doing some advertising, but we didn't have anything consistent. The excitement surrounding that game was tremendous."[58]

By coincidence, that was the same year Pilot Life surpassed $1 billion of life insurance in force.

"We had just celebrated those two things, the championship and the $1 billion mark, and I was looking for something real big and exciting to get the company involved in," Andrews said. "The day after that victory, I went up and talked to our president, O. F. Stafford, who was a great man."[59]

Andrews proposed that Pilot Life sponsor an Atlantic Coast Conference (ACC) basketball schedule. Stafford, who like everybody else near a television had watched the game the night before, agreed and told Andrews to work something out. Over the next months, Andrews worked with a sports producer to convince universities that they wouldn't lose spectators if the games were televised. By the fall of 1957, Pilot Life had put together an initial twelve-game schedule of ACC basketball. Even better, Pilot Life was the sole sponsor and only advertiser.

"The other companies didn't think we were ready for that kind of entertainment advertising," Andrews said. "But it went over just great."[60]

Pilot Life's next challenge was filling its new advertising time; each commercial was one full minute. The company's advertising agency developed a theme song called "Sail with the Pilot." The catchy jingle caught on, and through the 1960s it was a staple of high school and college sporting events in North Carolina.

"There were high school bands playing it, and we had sheet music," Andrews said. "It just went over tremendously. After we got the ACC thing going real good, more advertisers began to come on."[61] By the 1960s, Andrews began to look for other sponsorship activities. Before long, Pilot Life was sponsoring Southeastern Conference and Southwest Conference football and basketball. The company also began advertising in national magazines such as *Time*, *Look*, *Life*, and *Newsweek*.

Before long, Pilot Life did a survey to find out how well its advertising was working. The survey was extremely gratifying: It showed that Pilot's "Pilot at the wheel" logo was the most recognizable insurance company logo in the Southeast with the exception of Prudential's "The Rock."

Advertising alone could not account for Pilot Life's success in the 1960s. The company also became involved in a new government program called Medicare. Like Social Security, which had helped the insurance industry in the 1940s,

JEFFERSON-PILOT COMMUNICATIONS

BETWEEN THE 1940S AND THE 1960S, Southeastern Broadcasting (later Jefferson Standard Broadcasting) thrived under Joseph Bryan, its founder and president from 1934 to 1963.

In the 1940s, Bryan boosted WBIG's radio signal in Greensboro and hired former newspaperman Edney Ridge. Ridge soon became known as "Mr. WBIG." Listeners awoke to Arthur Godfrey and Jack Benny and went to bed listening to Amos 'n' Andy.

In the same period, Bob Poole left a lucrative career with the Mutual Broadcasting Network in New York to become WBIG's well-loved announcer. The gruff-voiced DJ dialed up the airport meteorologist every morning, and together the two gave a light-hearted local weather report. Every morning, city residents called WBIG to ask Bob, "Is it really going to snow?" or "Which high school team won the game?"[1]

When television began to upstage radio's popularity, WBIG increased its emphasis on music; the station had its own music director and a 10-musician orchestra. In the early 1940s, Maynard and Lance Spencer played mandolin and guitar, respectively.

WBIG also played a key role in two of the area's most devastating health crises. Greensboro was just recovering from a difficult experience with tuberculosis when polio struck in 1948. North Carolina was one of the most infected areas in the country, with 2,500 victims, and Greensboro was one of the state's hardest-hit cities. Guilford county was declared an epidemic area, and the American Red Cross made a nationwide appeal for help.

WBIG was well positioned to spearhead a statewide fundraising campaign to build a desperately needed polio center. The station partnered with the Greensboro News Company to raise $170,000, more than half the total raised in the state. "The People's Hospital" was built in 95 days, thanks to plenty of volunteer labor and donated supplies. Formally named the Central Carolina Convalescent Center, it was the nation's second-largest polio hospital.

WBT Radio

Always looking for opportunities to build Southeastern Broadcasting, Bryan found one in the mid-1940s. In 1945 he proposed to buy WBT-AM, a CBS-owned station in Charlotte, North Carolina.

The proposal seemed strange at first because WBT-AM had never turned much of a profit. The station signed on the air in 1922 with a 100-watt signal. According to Ned Cline's biography of Joseph Bryan, that first broadcast originated from Fred N. Laxtton's basement in Charlotte, North Carolina. The receiver was located in a nearby garage that, rumor had it, also housed chickens.[2] In 1929 CBS bought WBT radio and increased the power to 25,000 watts, enabling it to reach Cuba and the Bahamas. CBS announcer Grady Cole became so popular that Collier's magazine dubbed him "Mr. Dixie." Local farmers and housewives tuned in religiously for his opinion on everything from politics and the weather to the price of eggs.[3]

In 1945, however, CBS wanted to buy stations with signals that overlapped Charlotte. To comply with FCC regulations, it would have to divest itself of its radio stations in certain areas, including WBT.

The deal between Southeastern Broadcasting and CBS later made history. Bryan learned the most serious bidder for the station was the daily *Charlotte Observer*. Bryan and his station manager, Charles Crutchfield, were determined that the town's daily would not also own the radio station. Bryan learned that the *Observer* planned to bid $1.5 million, and he let it be known that he doubted anyone else would bid that high. Then he called Julian Price and told him, "If you'll just outbid $1.5 million, you can probably get the station." Price added exactly $5,000 to the *Observer's* bid—and bought a radio station.

On August 21, 1945, the FCC approved the transfer of WBT to Southeastern Broadcasting Company, with Bryan as its president. Southeastern changed its name to Jefferson Standard Broadcasting Company on January 11, 1947.

WBT soon became a fixture in North Carolina. Sisters Maybelle and Sara Carter and Sara's husband, A. P. Carter, were regulars—on their way to becoming the nation's most influential group in country music. The station was so popular that some weeks, 10,000 letters poured in from avid listeners who felt deep connections with its disc jockeys and live concerts.[4]

Throughout the 1940s, an old-time string band called the Briarhoppers sang for an audience of 450,000, under the sponsorship of the Pilot Life Insurance Company. They often visited Pilot headquarters and brought the Pilot name into the community as they played for crowds in the state's churches, schools, and community centers.[5]

In 1948, Jefferson purchased another station, WBT-FM. Its call letters changed to WLNK in 1997.

Television

Although he built Jefferson Standard Broadcasting on radio, Bryan continuously watched the development of television. He had been to New York in the early 1940s and had seen the crowds of people gathered around hotel televisions to watch the World Series baseball games.

When he returned a few years later, television antennas were everywhere, sprouting from roofs in residential neighborhoods and urban areas alike.

In February 1949, the nation's first daily TV newscast debuted; three months later, the *CBS Evening News* kicked off. Before long, Bryan obtained the first television license issued in North Carolina. At noon on July 15, 1949, WBTV signed on from Charlotte. With a transmitter on the top of Spencer Mountain in nearby Gaston County, it was the state's only television station.[6] One week later, WFMY-TV, owned by the *Greensboro Daily News*, gave its first broadcast.

Bryan's intuition about the new medium's potential was correct: When WBTV went on the air in 1949, there were only 1,000 televisions in the Charlotte area. One year later, there were 19,000.

In September 1950, Carolinians saw their first live network television program: a football game between Notre Dame and the University of North Carolina. In 1951, WBTV brought to the air a musician who was already charming audiences in WBT radio: Fred Kirby, the singing cowboy.

But turning a profit remained a steep climb: in the early years, WBTV lost as much as $50,000 a month, and Bryan's penny-pinching oversight of the station did not win him friends. In time, however, television advertising boomed, and the medium overtook the country. In the early 1950s, WBTV was the first in the Carolinas to offer color TV (at a time when *The Wonderful World of Disney* stood out against the black-and-white of news and other programming). Today WBTV continues operation as the flagship of the company's communications properties and remains a CBS affiliate in Charlotte.

With this success under his belt, Bryan continued to expand the company's reach into television, adding WBTW in Florence, South Carolina, and a station in Richmond, Virginia.[7] As the new stations were acquired, teams from Jefferson Standard Broadcasting went out to introduce them to the Jefferson Standard culture and position them in their respective communities.

The "Sail with the Pilot" sheet music was given free to band directors who wanted to teach their high school and college marching bands the popular tune. Partially because of this song, Pilot Life had the second-highest name recognition in the region, behind only Prudential.

Medicare was designed to help the elderly. It provided fee-for-service medical care for elderly people who were no longer covered by traditional employer-based healthcare programs. At first, Andrews remembered, insurance companies viewed Medicare as competition. But when it was clear that Medicare would soon become law, Pilot Life won the contract to offer healthcare insurance for North and South Carolina.

Bette B. Johnson, who joined the company in 1947 and eventually rose to second vice president of group sales administration, said Pilot Life had to expand the Group Department's office because "Medicare claims grew totally out of proportion."[62]

Ultimately, Pilot Life only held the Medicare contract for three years, said Craig McIntosh, controller of Pilot Life from the 1950s until 1980. "I think the main reason we took it is because we wanted to be on the inside," McIntosh said. "There was a big push for government to go into health insurance. But, in my opinion, it wasn't worth our time because it was too much trouble."[63]

Taken together, these factors pushed Pilot Life further and faster than at any other time in its history. In 1965, on its way to $3 billion of insurance in force, Stafford announced the company's "greatest year," with sales of $625.6 million.

The Ljung Years

At Jefferson Standard, the sales effort throughout these years was directed by Karl Ljung (pronounced "Young"), whose tenure as head of the Agency Department corresponded to the presidency of Chick Holderness: 1950 until both men retired in 1967. Ljung's vitality, intelligence, and no-nonsense style as director of the sales department are considered a crucial part of Jefferson Standard's success during the period. Yet as linked as were their careers, no two men could have been more dissimilar in background. Whereas Chick Holderness was born to the executive suite of an established and important Southern company, Karl Ljung was the son of a Swedish immigrant orphan.

Karl Ljung's father was one of a group of 50 boys brought to the United States by the Masons in the latter part of the 19th century. He was eight years old. After arriving in New York, the boys were put on a train to Chicago, where they were to be adopted by American families. Karl's father, however, got separated from the group in Chicago and was never found by the group leaders. He wandered about the city unable to speak English. He later would tell Karl that he had a nickel in his pocket, with which, out of curiosity, he bought a tomato, something he had never seen. He didn't like it.

Finally, the eight-year-old orphan spotted a sign in Swedish over a door. It told him there was a bakery inside, and the family that operated the bakery took him in. He had found a home. In 1898, still a young man, Karl's father enlisted in the U.S. Army to fight in the Spanish-American War. It was America's entry onto the international stage, and Ljung was wounded in what has come to be known as the Battle of San Juan Hill. After the war he was sent by the army as a recruiter to Goldsboro, North

Carolina, where Karl was born. When Karl was two years old, his father took a job with the postal service in Greensboro.

Karl Ljung attended public schools in Greensboro, and in 1920, a recent high school graduate and still a teenager, he went to work for Jefferson Standard as a clerk. When he ran into the new clerk in a hall of the old Dixie Building, Julian Price demanded, "Who the hell are you?" When he was told, Price asked the lad where he thought he was headed. "Any way up," was the simple reply. Price liked that. Ljung's reputation as a man of few words was born. Ljung would later remark that he "had to work twice as hard and put in a lot of overtime because I didn't have a college education."[64]

Ljung spent his entire professional life with Jefferson Standard, a career that set a record for longevity when he retired as a senior vice president, agency operations, after 47 years. Ljung played a singular and aggressive role in increasing the number of states in which Jefferson Standard agents sold and serviced insurance policies. During Ljung's tenure, the number of states increased from 14 to

32, plus Puerto Rico and the District of Columbia, and the field force reached a total of more than 1,400 agents, 81 branch offices, and 170 district offices.

Throughout his tenure, Ljung was known as a man whose word could be trusted. Ben L. Tabor, manager of the Harrisburg, Pennsylvania, agency, wrote of Ljung that he was "one of the strongest men I have ever known. He has never agreed with an agent for the sake of just getting along with him."[65]

Seth Macon later wrote that Ljung was also "quick to recognize the agents' needs. He knew the agents needed a pension program and he got it for us. He knew that the renewal savings program was a great asset and he got it for us. He realized that an agent must make as large a first-year commission as possible in order to earn the proper standard of living. He also knew that if a man is to become financially independent in this business, he must have better than average renewals. He worked hard to get this for us."[66]

Ljung's approach—sympathetic but with no frills—characterized his performance as he continued to drive sales up during the 1960s. He traveled

The Briarhoppers were a popular band that performed on WBT radio in the 1930s and 1940s. The group was sponsored by Pilot Life Insurance and sometimes visited Pilot Life's headquarters.

This 1957 brochure, produced by Karl Ljung at Jefferson Standard, featured Mr. 4%, a popular incentive program at a time when Ljung was urging agents to increase sales.

more than any of his predecessors, listening to what the agents had to tell him and not interrupting them as they did so.

"He has been a man who would tell you, and tell you good," said Ben Tabor, "and he has also been a man who would listen and listen good."[67]

Holderness Steps Down

In 1960, Pilot Life's assets stood at $209.5 million, up $14.6 million for the year. Jefferson Standard's assets were at $620.5 million, up $35 million. Pilot Life was earning a 4.67 percent return on its assets; Jefferson Standard's rate of return was 5.27 percent. In 1960, Pilot Life agents sold $273.5 million worth of policies; Jefferson Standard agents had total sales of $229.9 million.[68]

At the end of 1965, Pilot Life President O. F. Stafford announced "the greatest year in our 63-year history." Assets rose to $298.4 million. Earnings were 4.81 percent. Policy sales for the year, Stafford said, were $625.6 million, "surpass-ing by $144,580,913 the previous year's high. It marked the first time in the company's history that sales exceeded $600 million."

Similarly, Holderness announced that Jefferson Standard's assets were $825.8 million, up from $780.3 million the year before, with a return on investments of 5.42 percent. "Sales of new individual life insurance by Jefferson Standard in 1965," Holderness continued, "reached an all-time high of $380,474,795. This was our fifth consecutive 'best year' in sales, and the second consecutive year that sales have exceeded $300 million."[69]

Stafford proudly told shareholders that Pilot Life "now ranks in the top 3 percent of the world's largest insurance companies." Holderness noted, "As measured by volume of ordinary life insurance in force, Jefferson Standard today ranks in the top 2 percent among the nation's more than 1,600 stock life insurance companies."[70]

At the end of 1967, Holderness achieved one of the highest national honors in life insurance: He was elected chairman of the Institute of Life Insurance, the public relations arm of the industry. At the same time he was chairman of the Life Insurance Medical Research Fund, chairman of the University of North Carolina Medical Foundation, president of the North Carolina Citizens Association, and vice president of the North Carolina Business Foundation. He served on the boards of Burlington Industries, Carolina Telephone and Telegraph, and Duke Power and was an elder of First Presbyterian Church in Greensboro. In June 1966, the year before he retired from the presidency of Jefferson Standard, the University of North Carolina at Chapel Hill, his alma mater, bestowed on him an honorary doctorate.

In 1967, after an enormously successful run, Howard Holderness announced his retirement. His honors, while a clear signal of accomplishment, were not what subordinates remembered most when they were asked about their retiring boss. In their eyes, Holderness had accomplished something much more important: He had learned the names of the people who worked for him and remembered them.

By that time, Jefferson Standard had 81 branch offices and some 1,400 agents from coast to coast.

"Holderness is able to call all of the managers and most of the agents by their first names," wrote Conrad Paysour, the long-time business editor of the *Greensboro Daily News.* "He visits from twelve to fifteen of the offices each year. Holderness is able, most of the time, to recall the names of wives."[71]

As Holderness retired, Jefferson Standard was once again looking for a leader. This time, the company turned to a dedicated investment man, someone who had risen through the ranks of Jefferson Standard's securities department. When the board

P. D. Gold, second from left, symbolically "passes the cane" to Karl Ljung, third from right. The cane was presented to Gold by the field force in 1912, when he was head of the Agency Department. Howard Holderness is third from left and Albert G. Myers is on the far left.

announced that Roger Soles was the new president of Jefferson Standard, the company once again had a president who would leave his mark on the insurance company, and Soles signaled from the beginning that his was an ambitious plan.

A Jefferson Standard agent. For almost seven decades, these agents delivered relief in times of need.

CHAPTER FOUR

A WISE INVESTMENT

1968–1980

The life insurance business is a 100-year transaction. People pay premiums for 50 or 60 years. Then the beneficiary might be getting a return for another 40 or 50 years. It's unthinkable to take undue risk with their money.

—Roger Soles,
CEO and President
1967–1993

ROGER SOLES CAME INTO the presidency at a crucial time. Growth for both Jefferson Standard and Pilot Life had been rapid throughout the 1950s and 1960s. By 1968, Pilot Life had, in fact, grown larger than Jefferson Standard in terms of insurance in force, yet the two remained emotionally and, more importantly, financially connected. Once again change was afoot, and Jefferson Standard and Pilot Life would have to adapt.

In this case, the change was economic. In the United States, economic growth had been steady from the end of World War II until the late 1960s. Heading into the 1970s, however, it began to slow. American military forces remained bogged down in the increasingly expensive and increasingly desperate war in Vietnam. At home, after decades of remaining steady, interest rates began to creep up, driven by inflation. Worst of all, two major oil shocks would upend the U.S. economy in the 1970s. The first occurred in 1972, the other in 1978. In both cases, the oil-producing states of OPEC either embargoed or threatened to embargo the shipment of oil to the United States. The result was the same each time: Fuel prices skyrocketed, and the economy ground to a halt.

At Jefferson Standard, Roger Soles looked over this landscape and knew that dramatic change was needed. He hired a consulting firm, McKinsey & Company, to help develop a strategic direction.

Fortunately, there was plenty of room for improvement with little disruption to the two companies' basic operations. Only a month after assuming office, at the August 1967 board meeting, Roger Soles announced an ambitious reorganization of Jefferson Standard and Pilot Life and their various subsidiaries. Shareholders approved the plan at a special meeting May 22, 1968, and it became effective June 26, 1968.

"Our new corporate structure is designed to deal with the rapid changes occurring in the field of financial services and affords an excellent basis for expansion and diversification of our operations," Soles said.[1]

The most fundamental change involved the creation of a new holding company, Jefferson-Pilot Corporation.[2] This holding company immediately became the parent organization of all Jefferson Standard and Pilot Life operations. Its subsidiaries included Jefferson Standard Life Insurance Company, Pilot Life Insurance Company, Jefferson Standard Broadcasting, and North Carolina Broadcasting.

The holding company made sense for a variety of reasons. Most immediately, significant tax

---

The Jefferson-Pilot Corporation logo. Jefferson-Pilot was created by Roger Soles in 1968 to take advantage of the significant tax and administrative advantages of being under one umbrella.

advantages accrued from grouping all the various companies under one umbrella. And beyond the taxation issue, Jefferson-Pilot realized a host of benefits, including (1) an expansion of corporate communications and training programs; (2) the opportunity to expand the company's product lines; and (3) administrative synergies, especially in the area of information processing.

"Jefferson-Pilot Corporation was formed in 1968 because of the adverse income tax consequences that we suffered. Tax laws penalized a life insurance company that owned another life insurance company," explained Robert Koonts, an attorney who worked for Ed Hudgins, Jefferson Standard's general counsel. Koonts later became general counsel himself. "So Jefferson-Pilot was formed, and I had the pleasure of preparing the charter, taking it to Raleigh, and filing it. I remember that very vividly."[3]

As he unveiled the new organization, Soles announced several other improvements in the company's operations: reorganization of the field force, enhanced staff services, greater agent compensation, and better managerial systems.

Increasingly Sophisticated

Each company's rationale for change represented an idea or trend whose time had come. Computers, for instance, had been a part of Jefferson Standard and Pilot Life's operations since the early 1960s. Yet these early and primitive machines were of little more use than punch cards. Even into the late 1960s, the cashier's office painstakingly typed every automatic draft for every premium collection, figuring interest on policy loans on paper and writing it on the premium cards.

By the late 1960s, however, computing power had increased dramatically, and it was clear that Jefferson Standard and Pilot Life would soon be able to store their huge amount of data on computers. At Pilot Life, John K. Jones was in charge of the ongoing project to upgrade computer systems.

Several members of the Pilot Life office staff pose in front of a mechanical card sorter. By the late 1960s, these machines were gradually giving way to new computers.

IBM employees take new mainframe computers into the Sedgefield office. These computers had enough power to save the entire company's files on disk.

When the company finally did get its new computers, the change resonated most deeply with company veterans like Archie Coleman, a World War II vet who lived on Jefferson Road and had worked for the company since the Great Depression. "One of the big things that made the company really start going was the computer thing," Coleman said. "They finally got it going where we had all the records on the computer and everybody had a computer at their desk. We could access anything."[4]

Jefferson-Pilot was becoming more sophisticated in other ways, too. Dick Andrews at Pilot Life was remembered as one of the first cross-company executives; he held influence at both Pilot Life and Jefferson Standard even when the companies were separate. Shuttling back and forth between the two, Andrews recognized that advertising was becoming more powerful and saw an opportunity at Jefferson Standard for more advertising. As the holding company was born, he suggested to Roger Soles that Jefferson Standard follow Pilot Life into television advertising. Seeing how effective advertising was, Soles agreed.

"Mr. Soles, wise man that he was, insisted that if we were going to continue to advertise, we had to do one spot for Pilot Life and one for Jefferson Standard," Andrews remembered. "Normally the TV stations would not even sell advertising like that. It would be two competitors, but we developed commercials for both Jefferson Standard Life and Pilot Life."[5]

Stafford Steps Down

Soles' ascendancy coincided with a general turnover in the executive suite. At Pilot Life, O. F. Stafford announced his retirement in 1967. He was

Rufus White with his pipe at Pilot Life's Sedgefield headquarters. White became president of Pilot Life in 1968 after rising through the sales and marketing side of the company. (*Photo courtesy of John Page*).

replaced by Rufus White, who was named the new president and CEO of Pilot Life in 1968. White was a native of Hertford, North Carolina, and had attended public schools there. He had joined Pilot Life as an agent in 1928 and risen through the agency side. In 1942, he was named manager, ordinary sales and administration, at Gate City. Three years later, during the merger of Gate City and Pilot Life, he became a supervisor for Pilot Life Insurance. From there, he gradually rose through the ranks, becoming senior vice president in 1964.

In 1971, Louis Stephens succeeded White as president. White continued to serve as chairman and CEO until 1973. Although his tenure as CEO was relatively short, White was remembered fondly.

"Insurance is a great business, with many challenges and opportunities," he later said. "In this industry, you can build a worthwhile career while helping individuals, families, business people, and corporations by making them more financially secure. This, in turn, adds to the security of the nation as a whole."[6]

Louis Stephens, White's successor, also came up through the ranks of Pilot Life—although like Roger Soles he came from the investment side of the company. After two years at Jefferson Stan-

dard, Stephens joined Pilot Life in 1949 to create a securities department. In 1965, he was named vice president and treasurer of the company.

"Things were growing and changing so much," Stephens remembered of his appointment as Pilot Life's president and chief administrative officer in 1971. "It was a very tough assignment, but the fact is, I had a group of very capable men and women, and they made it possible to carry the company on."[7]

Similarly, there was change at Jefferson Standard below the executive suite. In 1967, longtime agency manager Karl Ljung retired. Bob Taylor was named head of the Agency Department, but he retired in 1970. In his stead, Seth Macon, a longtime agency man, was named senior vice president, agency. Later, Macon recounted his ascendancy to the top marketing job at Jefferson Standard.

"Roger Soles called me into his office and said, 'Bob Taylor is retiring. I want you to be head of the agency department,'" Macon said. "I said to Roger, 'I'm not sure you want me in that job.'

"That surprised him a little bit, and he asked me why not," Macon remembered. "I said, 'Well, let me tell you something. Ed Hudgins, the head of your legal department, has been on the board for years. George Cavanaugh, the head of your investment department, has been on the board for years. Karl Ljung, the head of your agency department for the last twenty years, never made it to the board. In my opinion, the head of the marketing operation ought to be represented on your board of directors. You should appoint someone who is qualified to become a board member.'

"Roger was shocked that I took that position, but he said we should think about this over the weekend and talk about it on Monday. I didn't sleep a bit over the weekend, but he called me back on Monday morning and said, 'I've been thinking about this, and I think you are qualified to sit on the board, and we'll work toward getting you there.'"[8]

Although the reorganization represented changes to the corporate structure, operations within Jefferson Standard and Pilot Life continued to follow time-honored patterns. They remained independent companies with unique market profiles and dedicated sales forces. They still considered themselves the best of competition as well as the closest of friends. And they continued to grow quickly, despite the turmoil of the outside world. In 1967, Jefferson Standard passed the $3 billion mark of insurance in force and continued to move forward, reaching $4 billion in 1973, $5 billion in 1976, and $6 billion in 1978. During the same period, between 1968 and 1976, Pilot Life jumped from $4 billion in 1968 to $10 billion in 1976.

Roger Soles: The Leader

With the birth of the modern Jefferson-Pilot, Roger Soles began to project his personality and priorities into operations at Jefferson Standard and, in conjunction with Louis Stephens, Pilot Life. It was an especially trying time to be a financial services company, but it became apparent early on that Soles was a solid and capable leader. An early college graduate, he was enormously intelligent and "got to the core of the thing in a hurry," according to Jack Warmath, who worked alongside him for many years.[9]

Soles was also a dedicated investment man. He had come up in the securities side of Jefferson Standard, helping to build one of the nation's premier life insurance investment portfolios. His focus on sound investments would have long-term implications for Jefferson-Pilot's future.

A conservative investor, Soles was also known as a superior credit analyst. For example, in the 1960s and 1970s, Jefferson Standard invested heavily in daily newspapers through a subsidiary called JP Publications, which was formed in partnership with a businessman named Carmage Walls, a board member in the late 1970s.

This was an opportunity that most investment houses were only too happy to pass by. Daily newspapers, especially in the 1970s, were notoriously fickle in their finances, and they attracted lawsuits like "a fly to honey."[10] Roger Soles himself would later remark that "newspapers' balance sheets scare the average person to death."[11] Nevertheless, he saw potential, and Jefferson Standard made good investments in the newspaper market. When it came time to divest its newspaper holdings, the company made a substantial return.

"Roger Soles was an extremely innovative financier," said John Still, who joined Jefferson Standard's investment side in 1971. "He and Jack Warmath did some things that were just out-of-the-box thinking in the financial world. This company, for example, was a real leader in financing the newspaper industry. The newspaper business was beginning to consolidate out of family hands into these large corporate chains, and there were very few lending institutions that would finance newspapers because the values were intangible. Jefferson-Pilot was virtually the only source of long-term capital. We structured aggressive transactions that turned out to be very good deals in terms of performance."[12]

Personally, Soles was frequently described as a tough, fiercely competitive, and even intimidating leader—who nonetheless had a "heart of gold."[13] Molly Walls, who owned two newspaper companies with her husband independently of Carmage's partnership with Jefferson-Pilot, remarked, "There have been those who said he was stubborn as a mule, but the truth of the matter is, inside he's just a warm, fuzzy bear. He just doesn't want anybody to know it."[14] Molly herself joined the board of directors in 1990 and remained personal friends with Soles for many years.

Loretta Courson, an agent who joined Jefferson Standard in 1962, remembered a particular incident that showed Soles' personality. Every year, Jefferson Standard had a meeting at the famous Doral Country Club in Florida, where Soles golfed with the company's top producer. (In those days,

ROGER SOLES

ROGER SOLES WAS BORN IN 1920 IN TINY Whiteville, North Carolina. His father was a tobacco farmer who also grew corn and strawberries. Soles graduated from Whiteville High School as class valedictorian when he was only 14 years old. He went to Presbyterian Junior College in Maxton for two years and entered the University of North Carolina at age 16.

Restless, Soles left college before graduating and spent brief periods as a farm worker and as a clerk in a Whiteville department store. But as World War II began, Soles joined the Army Air Corps.

He trained as a combat navigator and was sent to the South Pacific as a lieutenant. There, Soles served for five years in the Army Air Corps, flying 100 missions, and was shot down while on a bombing run over the Solomon Islands. Soles and his crew members bailed out and spent two days on a deserted part of a Japanese-held island before they were rescued by an American submarine. Soles spent six months with the submariners and was later presented with the symbolic dolphins of the submariners.

After the war, Soles returned to Chapel Hill to study law. But as luck would have it, there was a delay, and Soles could not immediately enroll in law school. As he waited for classes to begin, he decided to take some courses in business management and accounting. He excelled in those classes, decided to stay with the program, and received a B.S. in commerce in 1947.

At the same time, Soles embarked on a modest enterprise. The story still circulates that Soles' "other enterprise" was playing poker and that he paid his way through college with his winnings. More believably, Soles simply began investing and found out that he was good at it. He made money, but not by raking it in from the middle of a table.

This combination of academic achievement and practical knowledge made Soles an attractive candidate for several companies. He was recruited by George K. Cavanaugh, the director of Jefferson Standard's brand-new securities department. Soles was 26 years old.

He went to work as a securities analyst in the spring of 1947, moving into an office on the Jefferson Building's 14th floor. Soles became assistant manager of the securities department in 1951; by 1959 he was manager. In 1962, he was elected vice president and in 1964 became assistant to Holderness. Two years later, he was named executive vice president.

When Holderness retired in 1967, he recommended Soles: "Since joining Jefferson Standard in 1947, Roger Soles has distinguished himself not only by his keen financial judgment and knowledge in the investment field, but also as a highly capable executive." The year before he became president, Soles earned the designation of Chartered Life Underwriter, making him among the few insurance company leaders to be a CLU.[1]

it was Jim Tice more often than not.) One year, while having coffee with Soles after golfing, Courson said to Soles, "You know, I'm going to take golf lessons up, and next year, I'm going to play you, and I'm probably going to beat you."

Soles looked over at her and said, "It will be the last damn time."[15]

His delivery was bone dry, but Courson—who knew Soles quite well by this time—recognized that he was joking. "He was always the first to call you and ask something," she said. "He would listen to you, and he would always do what was right. He really cared about the employees. He sincerely did. He would be the first not to take a raise and instead give the company employees a raise."[16]

Stories like this abound. Many of the people who worked most closely with Roger Soles say that his exterior could be gruff, but the roughness was only skin deep, perhaps even a calculated way to assert his leadership. Soles became president when he was only 46 years old, and he quickly embarked on the most ambitious reorganization of the two

Roger Soles, center, with his wife, Majelle, left, and their daughter, Jan, far left. The Soleses' daughter-in-law, Melanie, and son, William, are on the right. The family gathered for the 1990 dedication of the new Jefferson-Pilot building.

companies since their founding. He would have needed all the authority he could muster to keep control of the organizations.

Apparently it worked. Among the people who knew him best, Soles was revered for his acumen, his discipline, and his focus on growing the company. Although he wasn't widely known for flexibility, Soles' record as a leader showed real innovation and forward thinking. An evaluation of the reorganization was written fifteen years later, noting that Soles "saw the opportunity not only to respond to changing markets, methods, and procedures, but to reinforce the lines of business that were traditional with Jefferson Standard and Pilot Life."[17]

On June 9, 1969, almost a year after the creation of Jefferson-Pilot, the first shares of the new stock rode the Big Board at the New York Stock Exchange. Roger Soles was on hand to purchase the first 100 shares.

"These achievements were gratifying in those first years as a holding company to those who engineered, built, and adapted to it," said *The Jeffersonian* in August 1982, "as they must have been to the man who initiated it all."

Inside Jefferson Standard

Soles did not see reorganization as another way to conduct old business but as a way to enter new lines of business and hold Jefferson-Pilot steady. John Ingram, who joined Jefferson Standard's mortgage loan department in the mid-1970s, remembered Soles for providing a steady hand during a tumultuous time.[18] Inflation and rising interest rates proved the biggest challenges, but state and federal tax and regulatory authorities added to the pressure.

"When I came here, Roger had been the president for seven years," Ingram said. "He did a terrific job of guiding the company through those perilous times, and I think he was the right person for the company at the right time."[19]

Ingram's confidence is borne out by the figures. Jefferson Standard's 1967 annual report showed sales peaking at $406.2 million, pushing the company to $3 billion of insurance in force by year's end. Assets stood at $890.3 million. Jefferson Standard's net investment earnings rate was 5.21 percent. By the end of 1970, the company had improved the rate to 5.85 percent, and by 1975 the rate for earnings on investments stood at 7.22 percent.

"Even in those times, Jefferson Standard and Pilot Life were doing private placements, making commercial mortgage loans or residential loans that not a lot of the other companies were doing," Ingram said. "And, of course, we were operating in the South; the South was growing, so our business was focused in the South. Roger was very intuitive, a very good investor, and made the company a lot of money."[20]

During Soles' first full decade as president and CEO, Jefferson Standard's assets increased from $996.1 million in 1970 to $1.2 billion in 1975 and on to $1.6 billion in 1980. That growth was fueled by sales of new life insurance that grew from $366.2 million in 1970 to $523.5 million in 1975 and over the $1 billion mark in 1980. Reflecting the inflationary times, the average size of a new policy sold by Jefferson Standard agents grew from $10,568 in 1970 to $28,464 in 1980.[21]

Jefferson-Pilot Communications

During the reorganization, Soles created a special branch of the new corporation for Jefferson-Pilot Communications, the company's media operation. By 1970, Jefferson-Pilot Communications comprised two television stations and three radio stations. WBIG, the company's first radio station, remained its flagship media outlet and boasted a legend in radio broadcasting, Bob Poole.

"Poole did a coast-to-coast music show, Poole's Paradise, in New York City," remembered Lloyd Gordon, who was news director at WBIG for 28 years. "But he got tired of the New York rat race and came back to WBIG, where he had really started in radio."[22]

Meanwhile, a situation was brewing at the company's Virginia television station, WWBT. "The initial people who had been sent in to help make the transition had not exactly been successful in blending the station into the JP culture," remembered John Shreves, who joined Jefferson-Pilot Communications in 1971. "A small group of people were asked if they would move to Richmond and see if they could positively redirect it, and I was asked to go. I thought it was great fun and a huge challenge. We went there and successfully rebranded the station as WWBT and expanded its local news and its community focus. It became a success."[23]

Besides ownership in media outlets, Jefferson-Pilot Communications was changing in other ways. As Dick Andrews at Pilot Life was noticing, television advertising became much more sophisticated and important in the 1970s. Yet most advertising agencies were still used to print media, and few had mastered the new medium yet. As a result, many television stations began to create small, in-house advertising agencies, much like the ones offered by magazines. WBTV, Jefferson-Pilot's station in Charlotte, founded an in-house agency

in the late 1960s. Even when the large advertising houses in New York began to offer better television advertising, these in-house agencies remained a less expensive alternative.

"Jefferson Productions, which was renamed Jefferson-Pilot Teleproductions in 1984, was created to make commercials primarily for the TV stations, but it developed into one of the top two or three commercial production companies in the country," said Ed Hull, who joined in 1970. "We were working for Coca-Cola, Proctor and Gamble, Ford, Kodak, and a host of *Fortune* 500 companies."[24]

Ever the entrepreneur, Bryan remained anxious to grow Jefferson-Pilot Communications through acquisition and was always looking for good deals. In 1974, he found two. That year, Jefferson-

Dick Andrews, left, and Louis Stephens, center, accept an award from Carl James, right, in 1977 after Pilot's 20th year of sponsoring Atlantic Coast Conference basketball.

Pilot Communications expanded with the purchase of WQXI (AM) and WSTR (FM) in Atlanta and KKFN (AM) and KYGO-FM in Denver, bringing the total number of stations to seven, four on the AM dial and three on FM. Clarke Brown, who would later become the president of Jefferson-Pilot's radio division, joined the company through the WQXI acquisition.

These new stations were followed shortly afterward by two more: WLYF (FM) in Miami and WGBS (AM), also in Miami. By 1980, Jefferson-Pilot

A Pilot Life ad in the 1970s shows the company's down-home and folksy image. In those days, Pilot's aggressive advertising made it one of the best-known names in the region.

Communications was fairly large, with nine radio stations in various markets across the United States, including AMs in Greensboro, Charlotte, Atlanta, Denver, and Miami, and FMs in Charlotte, Atlanta, Denver, and Miami.

Life at Pilot

Out at Sedgefield, Pilot Life continued to thrive, capitalizing on two decades of momentum. Originally a Jefferson Standard man who transferred to Pilot Life early in his career, Louis Stephens had come up in Pilot Life's relaxed, more folksy atmosphere.[25]

Stephens was concerned with growing Pilot Life's business, not with ruling with an iron fist. In those days, Pilot Life still had big divisions for group and individual health insurance, home service insurance, and ordinary life insurance. Over the

previous 20 years, the company had also built an enviable track record of youth marketing, following the baby boom generation from grade school into high school. By the 1970s, many baby boomers were in college—and Pilot Life once again sought a way to reach them by creating insurance products for sale by college-age kids to college students.

Sam Elkins graduated from college in 1968 and by 1970 was selling Pilot Life insurance to the newly christened "college market." This market was strong enough that Elkins made the prestigious Million Dollar Round Table of top-selling insurance agents his first year. "The college market was a whole life contract, or permanent insurance," Elkins remembered. "You showed them the premium, and Pilot Life was financing the college kids for a year until they got out of school."[26]

This focus on the college market, however, would last only a few years before the group would be disbanded and its agents moved to other markets. Baby boomers, now in their twenties, were evolving into a diverse group with wildly varied tastes and financial goals, and it was difficult to reach them by traditional insurance marketing routes.

It might be said, however, that the baby boomers' transformation was also America's transformation. In the 1970s, many of the social movements of the 1960s became mainstream. This trend was especially evident in the women's movement. In the 1970s, Pilot Life—a company with a long history of promoting women—named Mary Onn Parham its first female vice president. "Being the first to do something is typical of this company," Parham later said. "Since then, there have been several other female vice presidents."[27]

Elsewhere, Pilot Life continued to adapt to changing circumstances. Throughout the 1960s, Pilot Life had blazed trails with its advertising, sponsoring the ACC basketball schedule before corporate sponsorship of collegiate sports was known. Through one-minute ads written by a local agency, this sponsorship had given Pilot Life excellent name recognition throughout the South. By the 1970s, however, the situation had changed. Television advertising had been proven as a way to spread name recognition and sell insurance, and the advertising field was crowded. Pilot Life was no longer the sole sponsor of ACC basketball and found itself up against tough advertising competition. In response, Pilot Life switched to a much larger agency and worked harder on its own campaign.

"By the 1970s, I saw advertising from RJR, Liggett & Myers, Bank of America, and other companies," Dick Andrews remembered. "Our advertising didn't look as good to me when I saw our ads up against some of those from other companies. That pushed us to become much more critical of our own ads and much more professional in what we did with them."[28]

The divisions continued to evolve. For many decades, Pilot Life's Industrial Division, or Home Service division, could be counted on for stalwart growth. In the 1970s, this division, which had earlier changed its named to the Combination Division, changed its name once again, this time to Home Service. At the time, it was under the management of Dr. Frank Starr, senior vice president. Starr had begun with Pilot Life as medical director.

"By the time I came along in 1971, our original market, which was low-income people who often lacked bank accounts, had gotten very narrow," Starr said. "The number of people who needed home collection was declining. Our field force tended to be product and premium mode–driven as opposed to market-driven. Our market was narrower and narrower as we pursued this strategy. I hoped to turn the direction of that division so that we would be market-driven as opposed to product driven."[29]

Ultimately, this represented a major change in the division's traditional business. While Home Service agents continued to walk their beats collecting premiums, the division introduced new marketing strategies that widened its focus. New rates and policies were introduced, along with a new rate book and sales brochures, new training, and a dedicated advertising program.[30] Ultimately, the weekly premium business was discontinued.

Bob Martin, who began working in the Home Service division in the 1960s, remembered the 1970s as the division's heyday.

Louis Stephens, the seventh president of Pilot Life. He spent two years at Jefferson Standard before transferring to Pilot Life in 1949 to start the securities operation.

LOUIS C. STEPHENS

LOUIS STEPHENS GREW UP IN THE SMALL eastern North Carolina town of Dunn, 40 miles south of Raleigh. Dunn was once described as "the largest wagon cotton market in the Southeast." Stephens was the only son of a farming couple, and his early life was surrounded by cousins and filled with chores. His going off to the University of North Carolina at Chapel Hill to study accounting was not unusual for the only son of a prosperous farmer, but he demonstrated that his course was going to be unusual when he earned a Phi Betta Kappa key, graduated at the top of his class, and proceeded to the Harvard University Graduate School of Business Administration.

Despite having a scholarship, Stephens had to drop out of Harvard after a year to serve three years in the U.S. Navy. He served 20 months in the Pacific and was discharged as a lieutenant commander. He returned to Harvard to complete his master's degree. Upon graduation, he pondered what direction to take.

"I liked New England, and I think I could have been happy working there," he later said. "But I liked North Carolina better. So I came home and went to see Dean Dudley Carroll [dean of UNC's School of Commerce] for advice about where in the state to look for a job."

Carroll recommended that Stephens visit Jefferson Standard, where, after a conversation with Joe Bryan, he decided to stay. In 1947, Stephens went to work as a securities analyst in the investment department. In 1949, he joined Pilot Life to organize and direct its securities department. He remained with Pilot Life for 38 years, gradually moving up the executive ladder to president.

"We had probably 600 agents back then," Martin said. "In those days, people were not as quick to use postal facilities or bank drafts as they are today. People were paid weekly, so the agents collected the premiums weekly, frequently walking their routes in the city. The home service districts were focused on marketing to workers in the South's major businesses of textiles, furniture, tobacco, and agriculture."[31]

In the investment arena, Stephens stayed true to his roots and built an enviable operation.[32] In 1968, Pilot Life's earnings rate on assets of $379.6 million was 5.22 percent. By 1971, that rate improved to 5.98 percent, and by 1975 the rate was 7.43 percent. During that same period, assets grew from $436.5 million in 1970 to $658.6 million in 1975 and to $996.7 million in 1980.

In 1978, Pilot Life celebrated its 75th anniversary. Financially, the company had never been better positioned, despite the uncertainties in the national economy. In a special 75th anniversary magazine, Pilot Life boasted that it had more than $12 billion of insurance in force, 875 home-office employees, and 1,300 field representatives. To celebrate, Pilot Life threw a party at Sedgefield, offering games and rides for employees' children and speeches from President Louis Stephens, the mayor of Greensboro, and the governor of North Carolina.

"We are fortunate to have a favorable climate for increased sales and sound growth," Stephens wrote in the 75th anniversary magazine. "Innovations are taking place in our company today—in the home office and the field—that would have been unthinkable only a decade ago. We are keeping abreast of what is happening in our industry, and we actively seek changes that can be incorporated into our daily operations to the benefit of our policy owners, future clients, field representatives, staff, and stockholders."[33]

In his article, Stephens set ambitious goals for Pilot Life's future:

- Grow premium income from $316 million in 1978 to $582 million by 1982
- Grow Ordinary premiums from $68 million in 1977 to $94 million in 1982
- Grow Group premiums from $225 million in 1977 to $462 million in 1982

"Our future is bright," he declared. "Let us pledge to ourselves and our family that we can and will work harder to seek and sell more people that they can place their trust with Pilot Life."[34]

The Birth of Universal Life

It was a testament to the management of the various Jefferson-Pilot companies that they were in such sound financial health at the end of the decade. Tossed by oil shocks and recession, the 1970s were the most financially difficult years since the end of World War II. Many companies, especially those that depended heavily on investments, declared bankruptcy. By contrast, Jefferson Standard and Pilot Life both experienced gains approaching 8 percent in their investment portfolios.

At the end of the decade, however, 8 percent wasn't what it used to be. Between 1977 and 1979, the U.S. economy suffered through a strange economic phenomenon dubbed "stagflation," an unprecedented period of inflation during recession. As a result of the inflation, interest rates shot up to 15 percent for certain kinds of loans.

These high interest rates were devastating to the life insurance industry, which found itself competing with banks and other financial institutions that could promise much better returns. Something had to be done, and it wasn't long before the stress produced a real innovation: universal life insurance.

"Universal life insurance, which is basically a floating-rate product, was invented as a means of protecting the life insurance industry," said John Still. "It was a really seminal, pivotal event."[35]

The path was fraught with pitfalls, however. First, it was much more difficult to make money with universal life insurance because the rate of return varied depending on certain external factors. Second, some companies overextended themselves by offering single-premium life insurance policies based on sustained high interest rates. This strategy was dangerous in the long term because if interest rates fell, the insurers would be saddled with long-term liabilities that could not be matched by available returns on investments. That very thing would happen in the 1980s.

Jefferson Standard and Pilot Life, however, were not among the reckless. They continued to make excellent investments and to introduce new products carefully. While other financial institutions ran toward junk bonds and real estate as a way to revitalize portfolios that had been ravaged by high interest rates, Jefferson Standard and Pilot Life stayed away. As a result, by 1979, the year of the Iranian hostage crisis and widespread economic unrest, Jefferson Standard and Pilot Life were among the most financially sound life insurance companies in the country.

The Jefferson-Pilot building, in downtown Greensboro, opened in 1990.

CHAPTER FIVE

JP RISING
1981–1993

We wanted to be a good company to do business with. We wanted to treat our customers fair, give them good service. We wanted to take care of our employees, which we did, and most of them were happy. We wanted to be good corporate citizens, which we certainly were.

—Roger Soles, CEO and President, 1967–1993

JEFFERSON-PILOT EMERGED FROM the 1970s in excellent financial shape. The company and its subsidiaries had invested wisely and grown sales through one of the worst decades in American financial history.

Not all insurance companies could say the same. By the 1980s, the industry was changing. Universal life insurance, which offered the consumer a fluctuating interest rate that reflected the currently prevailing interest rates in the marketplace, was becoming more popular as insurance companies competed with stock brokerage and investment houses for customers. On the investment side, new financial tools began to appear on the market, especially a form of financing known as junk bonds. Many insurance companies flocked to the potentially lucrative bonds as the real estate market foundered.

"In the past decade," noted *The Jeffersonian,* "the United States has experienced an unprecedented rise in the rate of inflation accompanied by high interest rates. The insurance industry has suffered punitive taxes and regulatory problems. There have been many times that tried the mettle of every financial executive in the nation."[1]

The mettle at Jefferson-Pilot, however, proved stronger than most. In 1981, Jefferson-Pilot's earnings per share rose to $4.60 from $4.22. More than half of the company's earnings came from Jefferson

Standard, which boasted $6.7 billion of insurance in force.[2]

This was significant because Jefferson Standard was significantly smaller than Pilot Life, which boasted sales of $4.2 billion that year and total insurance in force of $20 billion. About 25 percent of Pilot Life's sales were home service, group insurance, and health insurance, and the rest derived from the Ordinary Department, or regular life insurance.[3] At the time, Pilot Life's agency system was under the management of Ralph Seigler, a senior vice president and longtime Pilot Life employee. The Home Service division was managed by Dr. Frank Starr until he retired in 1984.

Even with $20 billion of insurance in force, President Louis Stephens pointed out, Pilot Life had room to improve. "A turbulent economy, high levels of unemployment and intensely competitive industry conditions presented a challenging environment to our operations," he wrote. "These factors, combined with the continued rapid escalation of medical care costs, produced results less than planned."[4]

Even into the 1980s, the venerable Pilot remained a well-known icon throughout North Carolina and the South one of the most trusted names in life and health insurance.

Fortunately, the U.S. economy would recover by 1983 and gain strength throughout the decade. In 1984, the combined income from Pilot Life and Jefferson Standard reached $127.7 million. Sales of individual life insurance increased 11.2 percent, and life insurance in force hit a record $37 billion.[5]

Plainly the holding company was holding its own in turbulent times. In mid-1986, the American Council of Life Insurance issued a survey of consumer attitudes toward insurance companies. The report was aimed at gauging the public's acceptance of new products and services. An internal document reported highlights from the study: "After declining from 87 percent in 1968 to 76 percent in 1983, the proportion of respondents who choose life insurance as the preferred product for protection against premature death of a breadwinner has risen to 80 percent. . . . There have been significant declines over the past ten years in the number of people who claim to have difficulty with various aspects of life insurance. These areas include: understanding policy wording, determining how much to buy, figuring out policy costs, and deciding what type of policy to buy."[6]

Jefferson-Pilot Communications

Although it was much smaller than the insurance subsidiaries, Jefferson-Pilot Communications, under President Wallace J. Jorgensen, remained a solid contributor to earnings and an important part of the overall company strategy. As Jefferson-Pilot Communications' executives frequently pointed out, every time a viewer or listener heard the name "Jefferson-Pilot" on a television or radio station, or in conjunction with a sports event, the company's name spread a little further. The 1980s would bring important new growth, both for the radio and television stations and for the in-house production agency, Jefferson-Pilot Teleproductions.

In 1982, Jefferson-Pilot Teleproductions came across an offer that was too good to refuse. Pilot Life and Jefferson Standard had been advertising during Atlantic Coast Conference (ACC) basketball games for about 20 years. In fact, Pilot Life had sponsored the first televised broadcasts of ACC games. Yet the broadcast rights were retained by other companies. In 1982, however, Jefferson-Pilot Teleproductions had the opportunity to purchase the broadcast rights for ACC basketball.

"Before 1982, ACC basketball had been with Castleman D. Chesley and Billy Packer," remembered Ed Hull, who had been working for Jefferson-Pilot Teleproductions since the 1970s and later became president of Jefferson-Pilot Sports. "But Chez, as he was called, was getting out of the business for health reasons. We had production expertise to televise the games, so we had the opportunity to join with the ACC and Raycom out of Charlotte and get the broadcast rights for ACC basketball."[7]

It was a perfectly timed opportunity. ACC basketball already was one of the premier collegiate sports attractions.

"Oftentimes, ACC basketball would dominate a market so completely that 50-plus percent of the viewers would be watching those games," Hull said.[8]

At the same time, cable television was still struggling to get off the ground, and Jefferson-Pilot Teleproductions began selling broadcast rights to a start-up channel called ESPN the year after it was founded. The relationship with ESPN would grow, along with the cable sports channel's massive success.

Two years after the ACC basketball deal, Jefferson-Pilot Teleproductions saw another opportunity unfolding. In 1984, the College Football Association (CFA) deregulated college football. This move allowed each conference to handle its own syndication rights. As a result, Jefferson-Pilot Teleproductions soon acquired the syndication rights for ACC college football, this time acting alone.

This deal was followed in 1986 by the acquisition of the broadcast rights for Southeastern Conference (SEC) basketball, which had been on Turner cable. Then in 1988, Jefferson-Pilot Teleproductions put together a made-for-TV alliance that syndicated college sports in the northeast, including sports powerhouse Notre Dame the first year, in addition to Boston College and Rutgers. Finally, in 1992, Jefferson-Pilot Teleproductions bought the broadcast rights to SEC football.

Together, these four major sports packages commanded a wide audience and established

Opposite: The building that housed WBIG, one of Jefferson-Pilot Communications' original broadcasting stations. Inset, the transmitting antenna after it came down in 1987.

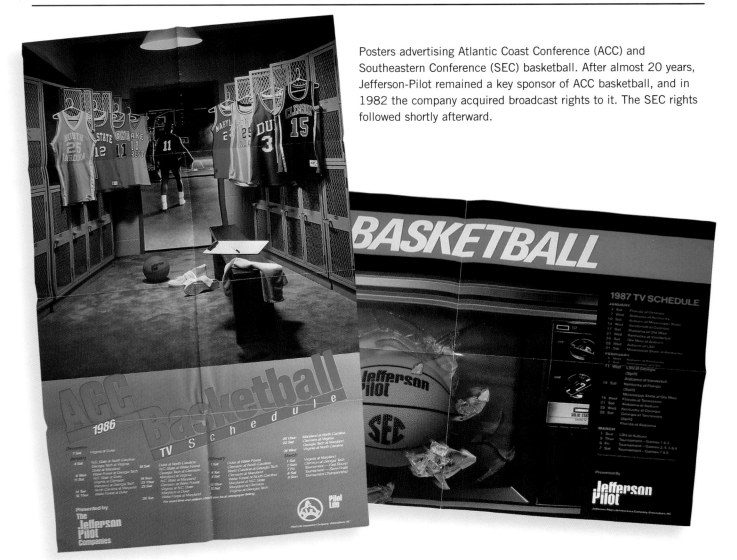

Posters advertising Atlantic Coast Conference (ACC) and Southeastern Conference (SEC) basketball. After almost 20 years, Jefferson-Pilot remained a key sponsor of ACC basketball, and in 1982 the company acquired broadcast rights to it. The SEC rights followed shortly afterward.

Jefferson-Pilot Teleproductions, which was renamed Jefferson-Pilot Sports, as one of the nation's premier syndicators of college sporting events.

Drawing on this experience, Jefferson-Pilot Sports began looking for additional broadcast opportunities, and in the mid-1980s it hit upon a perfect deal. At that time, stock car racing sponsored by National Association of Stock Car Auto Racers (NASCAR) was beginning its meteoric rise as a popular American sport, a transformation that took it from the Carolinas and the South to a nationwide audience. Hoping to capitalize on the sport's growing appeal, Jefferson-Pilot Sports signed a deal to broadcast the races at the Charlotte Motor Speedway in Charlotte, North Carolina. The company even helped create a Winston Cup NASCAR event at the speedway.

In time, however, the "price of poker" got too high, and Jefferson-Pilot Sports sold the national broadcast rights for the NASCAR event. The experience proved invaluable, however. Jefferson-Pilot Sports began pursuing other made-for-TV events, including a bicycle race called the Tour de Trump, made-for-television figure skating competitions (Ice Wars, Champions on Ice, and many others), and gymnastics events.

"All of these were sold to national television," Hull said. "We'd sell these events and actually create the television for them."[9]

Despite its high-profile events, Jefferson-Pilot Sports remained a very small part of the overall corporation—even a small entity within Jefferson-Pilot Communications itself. It was large enough, however, to effectively spread the Jefferson-Pilot name.

"That was always the goal," Hull said, "to get the name more national recognition."[10]

While Jefferson-Pilot Sports expanded, so did Jefferson-Pilot's Communication's portfolio of television and radio stations. By the mid-1980s, Jefferson-Pilot Communications was active in four markets: Charlotte, North Carolina; Miami, Florida; Denver, Colorado; and Atlanta, Georgia. The company had holdings in television, as well as AM and FM radio. In 1985, Jefferson-Pilot Communications expanded again, this time with the acquisition of two San Diego radio stations, KSON (AM) and KSON (FM).

"At the time, we were looking for growth markets," remembered Clarke Brown, who was sales manager in Atlanta during the acquisitions. "We wanted underdeveloped properties that could be turned around."[11]

To turn the San Diego stations around, Brown was sent to San Diego to help run them. From this acquisition until 1992, Jefferson-Pilot Communications did not open any new media markets. Instead, the company purchased radio stations in cities in which it already operated, including WAXY in Miami in 1991 and KCKK and KQKS (FM) in Denver in 1992.

The Merger

At the insurance companies, the financial trends first reported in the beginning of the decade were accelerating by the mid-1980s. In 1986, Jefferson Standard reported an increase in earnings of 8.5 percent while Pilot Life experienced a decline of 20.8 percent.[12]

The reason for this disparity was simple and obvious: health and group accident insurance. By the 1980s, the health care situation in the United States had changed dramatically. After decades of fairly steady and reasonable increases, the cost of health care was beginning to surge. Contributing factors included an aging population, new and expensive treatments, and rising costs of malpractice insurance. As a result, Pilot Life found itself subsidizing its health and group accident operations from its more profitable life insurance. For the short term, President Louis Stephens opted to keep the health and group accident lines until the future became clearer.

Much more important considerations were at hand, after all. By this time, Jefferson Standard and Pilot Life had been united under the same corporate umbrella for thirteen years, along with the Jefferson-Pilot Communications subsidiaries. And although they remained independent companies, they continued to move closer because of the many benefits of close operations. Computers, more powerful than ever before, penetrated deeper into the working environment, offering efficiency and savings at all levels. Similarly, it made sense to combine some investment and administrative operations.

In 1986, Roger Soles announced that his 20-year program of consolidation would finally reach its natural conclusion. As of January 1, 1987, Jefferson Standard and Pilot Life would be merged to create Jefferson-Pilot Life Insurance Company.

In 1987, Jefferson Standard and Pilot Life merged into one financial services and insurance company. Here workers remove the Jefferson Standard sign from the building in downtown Greensboro and put up the new JP signage.

The new company would offer the combined product lines of both Jefferson Standard and Pilot Life, including life insurance along with Pilot Life's operations in group insurance, credit life insurance, scholastic insurance, and home service.

In reality, Soles had been laying the groundwork for this merger for many years, and it was not a complete surprise to anybody. In an August 24, 1986, article in the *Greensboro News & Record*, business editor Jack Scism interviewed Roger Soles about the impending merger. He wrote, "Actually the formal merger of the two insurance companies is a continuation of a process begun several years ago, Soles noted.

"In recent years, investments, data processing, and product development have been consolidated, the life insurance policies of both companies are identical, Jefferson Standard agents have been selling Pilot Life's group and individual health policies, and Jefferson-Pilot Pension Life Insurance Company was created to serve the field force of both companies.

"'We had reached the point where we believed, to get further efficiencies, it was time to take the final step,' Soles said. 'Our challenge over the next year or two is to do that without any reduction in the momentum we have going.'"[13]

As Soles spoke, several aspects of the merger were already under way, including consolidation of support and service personnel; increased focus on marketing of new financial services; wider use of technology to achieve economies of scale; and, finally, an eye toward "more challenging opportunities."[14] In the legal department, company lawyers were working overtime to file in every jurisdiction in which Jefferson-Pilot operated. At the time, remembered General Counsel Robert Koonts, Jefferson-Pilot had offices in 37 states and Puerto Rico.[15]

While the companies merged relatively quickly, the distribution channels needed more time to become fully integrated. Jefferson Standard and Pilot Life had extensive agency operations throughout the country. In addition, Pilot Life had a brokerage operation that sold insurance through various independent agents.

Even though it would take a little longer for the distribution channels to merge, the benefits of the merger far outweighed the burden of work involved. In the advertising department, Jefferson Standard and Pilot Life completed the combination of their marketing that Dick Andrews had started years before, when stations ran one advertisement for Pilot Life and another for Jefferson Standard.[16] Shortly after the merger announcement, contracts were signed to televise 13 college football games on 18 television stations in several southeastern states. In addition, 37 college basketball games were to be televised on 30 major stations throughout the same area. Each telecast would include a minimum of four 30-second commercials featuring Jefferson-Pilot products and services.

Saying Goodbye to Sedgefield

The merger made sense in every way, but it was accompanied by at least one major change that would be emotionally difficult, especially for Pilot Life. In early 1988, slightly more than a year into the assimilation, Roger Soles announced that Jefferson-Pilot was building a new, 20-story Romanesque Revival office complex adjacent to the existing Jefferson Standard building in downtown Greensboro.

The new headquarters, Soles announced, would befit a major financial services and insurance company. It would include about 375,000 square feet of office space for 1,500 employees and an 800-car parking garage. The new building was designed "to retain the aesthetic beauty, the grace, charm, and tradition of the exterior" of the existing Jefferson Standard headquarters, Soles said. Twelve years earlier, the original headquarters building, once the tallest building in the Southeast, had been included on the U.S. Department of the Interior's National Register of Historic Places.[17] The total cost of the new building was estimated at $40 million.

When the new building was completed, it, along with the Jefferson Standard building, would serve as the headquarters for Jefferson-Pilot. While this step was necessary for the newly combined company to function at peak efficiency, it also meant that the 600 Sedgefield workers would be relocated

---

Opposite: The new Jefferson-Pilot building, designed to match the adjacent Romanesque Revival Jefferson Standard building, cost $40 million to build and stood 20 stories tall.

to downtown Greensboro. On December 10, 1986, Sedgefield workers were told that their sprawling, bucolic headquarters, built by A. W. McAlister six decades before, would be shuttered.

This move would be one of the hardest for Pilot Life's employees in the company's 85-year history—although there was wide consensus that it was necessary. "There were a lot of mixed emotions," remembered Joe Wheeler, a Pilot Life employee since 1964 and later assistant vice president of Jefferson-Pilot. "You get comfortable where you are, and all of a sudden, you've got to uproot and move."[18]

Over the years, Sedgefield had become synonymous with Pilot Life's operating culture. Ralph Seigler, agency manager and senior vice president, recalled sitting at his desk while the cherry trees bloomed outside. "I used to laugh and tell my friends that it's the only place in the world where I could sit in my office and have the cherry blossoms brought into my office by the wind," he said. "It's a beautiful setting."[19]

Many Pilot Life employees credited at least part of the company's unique culture to Sedgefield itself. Because it was located in the country, Pilot Life employees often carpooled or used a company bus, giving them a chance to socialize. And because of the buildings' sprawling layout, to travel from one department to another, employees had to walk through crowded work areas.

"You got to know people because you saw them all the time," remembered Randy Macon, who was in advanced sales at Pilot Life. "Everybody knew everybody else because of that."[20] By contrast, the new building was "straight up and down," with elevators depositing employees directly into their departments.

Opposite and right: In conjunction with the move, Pilot Life's much loved home at Sedgefield, opposite, would be closed and its employees moved downtown. It was a difficult transition for Pilot Life employees, who had formed a strong, emotional bond with Sedgefield. At right, 1950s-era employees availed themselves of the company's shuttle service. Touches like this and the office's open floor plan created a warm culture in which many employees knew each other.

"Unless you happened to run into somebody on the elevator, you might never see them," said Nancy Elkins, who worked for Dick Andrews in Pilot Life's communications department.[21]

Gone also was Pilot Life's more relaxed dress code. While at Sedgefield, men weren't required to wear suit and tie every day, and few of the officers wore suit coats every day. In the financial district downtown, it was necessary to dress more formally.

Sedgefield had also become the spiritual home of Pilot Life. Over the years, thousands of employees had worked and socialized at the headquarters, their children and spouses joining them on the weekends at Pilot Life's recreation facilities.

"We had jobs, but we also had fun," remembered Bert East, a longtime Pilot Life employee. "We had a square dance club, and there were swimming lessons and tennis lessons, Easter egg hunts for the children, New Year's Eve parties, and breakfasts and trips. The ladies' club went on trips to the beach, to Las Vegas, and to Canada."[22]

The move also meant another change of leadership. Louis Stephens, who had risen to the leadership role at Pilot Life at approximately the same time as Roger Soles had at Jefferson Standard, announced his retirement. Stephens had worked at Pilot Life since 1949. He had been president since 1971.

"I am proud that Pilot Life has competed effectively in a tough market," Stephens wrote in his final message to employees. "We have an outstanding record of growth in assets, insurance in force, and company profits. Our return on equity speaks well for the company and our position in our industry. But what gives me the greatest pride is our people. I've seen you produce, grow and blossom. I've seen you become very successful people.

"I take special pride in the team that we've built here. You are a quality crowd of people with integrity and good will. You have a healthy respect for each other and your company. There is a very special camaraderie and good spirit throughout our organization that I consider unique."[23]

Stephens left many admiring employees who had cherished their years working with him. "He was very dynamic," remembered Sam Elkins, a top agent for Pilot Life. "He always had a large influence because he was so easy and sensible, and he would listen."[24]

Roger Soles and other senior executives were sensitive to the tremendous change Sedgefield's closing and Stephens' retirement required of the corporation. Even before the merger was announced, the two companies' human resources departments got together and set up a joint-company team to walk to raise money for charity.

"We had a tremendous time," remembered Nancy Elkins. "Everybody wore the same JP T-shirts. That was the first thing we did together as a team, and we raised a lot of money together."[25]

Other opportunities for bonding soon followed. The Jefferson Standard day camp was open to Pilot Life kids, and the Jefferson Choraliers, a locally known singing group, was open to Pilot Life employees. The first year after the merger, the newly expanded and renamed Jefferson-Pilot Choraliers performed at a Christmas luncheon, and "everybody was amazed at how good they were," remembered Elkins.[26] Afterward, Roger Soles got up and said, "See, that's how good we can be when we work together."[27]

Heading into the 1990s

It would be many years before employees stopped identifying themselves as "Pilot" or "Jefferson" people. The financial benefits of the merger would materialize much more quickly. The company had made it through the 1980s with a solid record of growth and increasing returns on investments. This achievement was all the more remarkable considering the general state of the insurance industry. During the decade, several high-profile insurance companies declared insolvency, partially because of risky underwriting and partially because of bad investments. Junk bonds turned out to be unsafe investment vehicles. Worse yet, the real estate market nationwide suffered a protracted meltdown in the first half of the 1980s, severely devaluing investment portfolios across the country.

While it wasn't immune, Jefferson-Pilot nevertheless prospered, continuing eighty years of solid growth. If there was any complaint by 1990, it was that Jefferson-Pilot was a little too successful. The company was cash rich, making it a target for acquisition. Moreover, some shareholders felt that Jefferson-Pilot should be returning profits to the shareholders more aggressively.

Roger Soles, however, wasn't worried about the threat of acquisition and pointed out that shareholders had benefited tremendously over the past two decades. In 1990, the company earned $4.41 per share, a 20.8 percent rise. Sales of investments and net of income taxes accounted for 52 cents per share. If the effect of taxes were excluded, Jefferson-Pilot had earned more on straight operations than at any time in its history.[28]

These figures flew in the face of dire predictions about the insurance industry. "The financial condition of the life insurance industry came under heavy scrutiny in 1990," reported *JP Life Magazine*. "Hardly a day went by without a newspaper, magazine or broadcast story about the insurance solvency issue. As 1991 begins, this focus on insurer health is expected to intensify, in view of the state of the economy, the financial condition of banks, and increased congressional scrutiny of the way the industry is regulated. While Jefferson-Pilot, whose outstanding investment results rated among the top in the industry, escaped the controversy which faced many other major insurers, nonetheless the company was and continues to be affected by the atmosphere surrounding the industry."[29]

The atmosphere was created by what the American Council of Life Insurance called "a handful of companies" that "may have taken more risks than prudent." Regulators were concerned about the solvency of those companies, investors were looking for safer prospects, and consumers were confused by all the bad news. Junk bonds, poor real estate investments in the Southwest, and delinquent mortgage loans were all causing problems, the council said.

Jefferson-Pilot leaders did not disagree with the council's remarks; they simply replied by citing Soles' remarks in Jefferson-Pilot's 1990 annual report. "The corporation's excellent progress . . . is the result of earnings advances in each of the major business segments except communications operations," Soles said.[30]

Soles Steps Down

Jefferson-Pilot was well positioned for whatever challenges were to come. In an interview with the *Greensboro News & Record*, Soles remarked, "I

Opposite: The grand rotunda of the Jefferson-Pilot building gleamed with brass, wood paneling, and marble, befitting a major financial services company.

don't think there is any doubt Jefferson-Pilot Life Insurance Company will be big enough to compete with anybody in the business. With our size, we can do anything the biggest companies can do, and we like to think we can do it better. We can offer as good or better products, we can offer field people just as good a career, and we can give more personal attention to our customers than the largest companies."[31]

In 1990, the holding company reported assets of $4.45 billion, up from $3.83 billion five years earlier. Net income per share was $4.41, up from $2.97 five years before, and income per share was $3.99.[32]

The numbers continued to rise over the next two years. At the end of 1992, the stock was priced at $48.13, compared with $4.12 in 1967, when Roger Soles took office. The company's market value had increased from $350 million to $2.5 billion over the same period, and insurance in force had grown from less than $7 billion in 1967 to more than $40 billion in 1992.

"The last year I was there, earnings grew 16.7 percent, and the stock price rose 27.8 percent," Soles later said. "Going back 25 years that I served, the stock price rose 14 percent compounded."[33]

With this impressive record behind him, in February 1993 Roger Soles announced his retirement. He had presided over a period of great uncertainty and great change. In the 25 years he ran the company, Jefferson-Pilot had been created and its subsidiary companies reorganized twice. Although Julian Price is often credited with building Jefferson Standard, Roger Soles certainly presided over the creation of the modern Jefferson-Pilot.[34]

Above: This photo was presented to Jefferson-Pilot in recognition of its 1991 Super Sponsor Contribution for the Salute Freedom Fireworks Finale Fun Fourth in Old Greensborough.

Opposite: In 1993, Roger Soles announced his retirement from the helm of Jefferson-Pilot. This picture is the last official Jefferson-Pilot portrait of Soles.

While Soles was satisfied with his record at Jefferson-Pilot, he later said that the transition was not unexpected or traumatic. "There wasn't any letdown in the company," he said. "I set that date about three or four years before I retired. My board knew what it was."[35]

Nevertheless, finding his successor would not be easy, and the board conducted a nationwide search. On September 1, 1992, the search paid off: David Stonecipher was named the new president-elect and CEO-elect of Jefferson-Pilot. Stonecipher was the first company leader to be recruited from outside the ranks of Pilot Life or Jefferson Standard, and he came to the office with a plan. As he set about building his team, Stonecipher made it clear that he had ambitious goals for Jefferson-Pilot.

The Jefferson-Pilot management committee in 1993. Pictured, front row, is Chief Executive Officer David Stonecipher; second row, left to right, Executive Vice President-Individual Operations Kenneth C. Mlekush; Executive Vice President and General Counsel John D. Hopkins; and Executive Vice President-Investments E. Jay Yelton; third row, left to right, President-Jefferson-Pilot Communications William E. "Bill" Blackwell; Executive Vice President and Chief Financial Officer Dennis R. Glass; and Executive Vice President-Group C. Randolph Ferguson.

CHAPTER SIX

A MARKET LEADER

1993–2003

As we move into the exciting twenty-first century, we plan to be a leader.

—David A. Stonecipher, Chief Executive Officer, 1999

IN THE EARLY 1990S, THE SEARCH to replace Roger Soles was the most important task before the board of directors. The board knew the next leader would have both a tremendous opportunity and a great challenge in guiding Jefferson-Pilot through the 1990s.

To help find the right candidate, the board retained a leading executive search firm, Heidrick & Struggles, which soon presented several names to the nominating committee. David Stonecipher was one of those names, and according to at least one member of the nominating committee, the decision was a fairly easy one.

"He was head and shoulders above the rest from the first time we interviewed him," remembered Jim Melvin, a board member since 1988. "His record and his breadth of knowledge of the industry were superb. He seemed to have more of a vision of where he thought the industry was going."[1]

Stonecipher took control of Jefferson-Pilot at an opportune moment. Thanks to Soles, Jefferson-Pilot's investments had grown, and the company had a great deal of cash on hand. It was one of the few insurance companies that could make that claim after the 1980s. Yet there was also some concern that Jefferson-Pilot had lost market share in the life insurance industry in recent years.

This combination—a cash-rich company with steady market share—made Jefferson-Pilot an attractive target for a takeover, and by 1993, this

seemed to be a very real possibility. After a bruising decade, industry analysts predicted that a wave of mergers and acquisitions would transform the life insurance industry in the coming years. Thus Jefferson-Pilot enjoyed a range of options. The company could simply wait until someone made a rich enough offer. Or it could seek to lead.

In a very important way, the presence of Stonecipher was an indication of the direction the board wanted to take. He was the first CEO to have been recruited from outside the company. He was the first actuary at the helm. And he soon made it clear how Jefferson-Pilot would face the future.

Shortly after he became president and CEO on March 1, 1993, Stonecipher released a vision statement: "Jefferson-Pilot will be a market leader in selected insurance, financial services, and communications businesses by building on our financial quality and reputation and the skills of our people while achieving superior, long-term results for shareholders."[2]

This strategy required a two-part approach. First, Jefferson-Pilot would need to energize

---

Beginning in 1993, Jefferson-Pilot Financial embarked on a growth spurt that moved the company into the top fifteen companies in the life insurance industry.

marketing and sales. The career agency network remained a bedrock of strength—but one that would be difficult to expand quickly—so Stonecipher looked for alternative ways to drive new sales. Jefferson-Pilot's distribution channels would have to expand dramatically.

The second part of the strategy would be to use Jefferson-Pilot's capital clout for strategic acquisitions. This made perfect sense: The life insurance industry was headed for a period of consolidation, and Jefferson-Pilot was financially strong. All that remained was identifying the right opportunities for smart growth.

A Proxy Fight

While the emphasis on marketing and sales was not new—Jefferson-Pilot's lineage included numerous dedicated sales leaders—one North Carolina magazine called the impending acquisition strategy a "sea change" for the conservatively managed insurance giant.[3] However, the strategy had plenty of precedents, reaching all the way back to Julian Price, who in his last big move had acquired Pilot Life and Gate City in one transaction.

At the time, it was only fitting that a new CEO would head down the same path as Julian Price. When Stonecipher joined Jefferson-Pilot, the company had been subject, for two successive annual meetings, to a proxy fight and litigation initiated by Louise Price Parsons and her husband, Don Parsons. Louise Parsons was the granddaughter of Julian Price and a significant shareholder of Jefferson-Pilot.

The Parsons contended, among other things, that Jefferson-Pilot had accumulated large amounts of underutilized capital, that its revenues were not growing adequately, and that certain stock compensation for senior managers had been improperly granted. The Parsons wanted to see the company declare a large extraordinary dividend.

Because a substantial amount of management's time and attention was being devoted to this dispute, and there was the prospect of its continuing through the third successive annual meeting in May 1993, David Stonecipher recognized that a first management objective was to resolve the dispute. A first step in that effort was in March 1993 when Stonecipher and Board of

Directors Chairman Robert Spilman hired John Hopkins, a senior partner at King & Spalding, a major Atlanta law firm, as the company's new general counsel and member of Stonecipher's new management committee.

In their first conversation about his duties, Stonecipher told Hopkins that he must find a way to bring the Parsons' dispute to a satisfactory resolution. A few days after this conversation, Stonecipher received a handwritten note from Louise Parsons in which she expressed a desire to meet with him and said she had heard things about him that reminded her of her grandfather, Julian Price. Hopkins and Stonecipher saw this as a very positive sign that the dispute might be settled and immediately launched a series of meetings that led to a satisfactory resolution and permitted management to focus on the business free of this distraction.

Interestingly, a centerpiece of the settlement was the adoption of a Statement of Corporate Governance Principles, in which the company agreed to have a substantial majority of independent directors on the board and on its most important committees.

In this regard, Jefferson-Pilot led the way on issues that became required in 2002 and 2003 in the Sarbanes-Oxley legislation and New York Stock Exchange requirements. Perhaps Louise Parsons was prescient in her reference to her grandfather, as Stonecipher led the company in putting its excess capital to good use in implementing its acquisition strategy over the next decade.

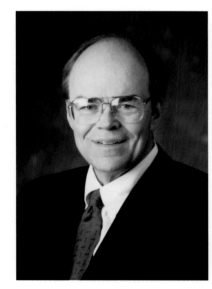

General Counsel John Hopkins was the second member to join Stonecipher's executive team. His first responsibility was to settle an ongoing proxy issue brought by a major shareholder and descendent of Julian Price. Throughout the mid- and late 1990s, he helped negotiate and close a string of acquisitions that transformed Jefferson-Pilot into a national company.

DAVID STONECIPHER

STONECIPHER GREW UP IN THE SMALL town of Cleveland, Tennessee, where he followed the path of many American kids, taking on a paper route when he was in seventh grade. Son of the manager of a chair factory, Stonecipher attended the private McCallie School in Chattanooga, Tennessee, and went on to Vanderbilt University, in Nashville.

He spent one summer working as an intern for Provident Life & Accident in Chattanooga, employing his skill in mathematics and getting his first taste of a career. "After my first summer in the business," he would say later, "I knew I had found my career. I have never been disappointed." His first love was math, and he would later tell an interviewer, "I learned that actuaries apply math to business situations. It's like the engineer of the life-insurance industry."[1]

Stonecipher graduated from Vanderbilt in 1962 after only three years. He spent two years in the U.S. Army and, upon discharge, went to work as an actuarial trainee with Life of Georgia. For the next twenty-eight years, he moved steadily up in the ranks and earned a master's degree in actuarial science from Georgia State University in 1967. At Life of Georgia, he was elected president and CEO in 1989. In 1991, he was elected CEO of both Life of Georgia and its companion company, Southland Life, as well as serving on the boards of Life of Georgia, Southland Life, Associated Doctors Health and Life Insurance Company and Georgia US Data Services, all subsidiaries of Georgia US Corp.

Stonecipher credits his experience with actuarial analysis— along with gaining knowledge of insurance products— for his managerial successes. "Ask anyone who has seen him scan several pages of figures and point out a discrepancy on page four," noted an observer in 1993, "and you'll know exactly what he means."[2]

About his coming to Jefferson-Pilot, Stonecipher tells the story of seeing a house in Atlanta that he especially liked and deciding he wanted to build one just like it in Greensboro. He did not know who lived in the Atlanta house but walked up to the front door nevertheless, determined to ask for a look around. The man who answered the door heard Stonecipher's story and, upon inviting him in, casually asked where it was he was planning to build. It turned out the man was an architect whose firm designed the Jefferson-Pilot building completed in 1990.

David and Nancy Stonecipher have four children: Stephen and Chris are his sons by a previous marriage, and Cathy and Angie are Nancy's daughters from a previous marriage.

The A-Team Assembles

Even as this issue was being resolved, Stonecipher concentrated on building his management team. In this, too, his timing was fortuitous because much of the leadership under Roger Soles was within a year or two of retirement. Robert H. Koonts, general counsel, retired in 1993 after a 44-year career at the company. Jack Warmath, Soles' chief investment officer, and Tom Fee, chief financial officer, took their retirements shortly thereafter.

Stonecipher would have an opportunity to rebuild the management ranks from the ground up without recriminations or hard feelings from disappointed veterans. "The transition was so positive and friendly," Melvin remembered. "There wasn't any 'I've got to get rid of you and you and you.' And Roger [Soles] never second-guessed David." In fact, Soles remained on the 14th floor for the last two years of his presidency despite the fact that new executive offices stood empty, awaiting his successor.[4]

Stonecipher's first hire, just prior to Hopkins as general counsel, was in 1992 when he hired Ken Mlekush as executive vice president. Mlekush was born and raised in Montana. He had started selling life insurance in 1961 as a way to supplement his income as a social studies teacher. In the first month, he made more money selling life insurance than in a year teaching, and he soon began selling insurance full time. By the time he was 35, Mlekush had risen into the executive ranks of Columbia National Corporation. In 1982, he joined Sun Life of America in Atlanta, where he served as senior vice president-marketing. In time, however, Sun Life announced plans to relocate to Los Angeles, a prospect that Mlekush's family did not like.

Fortunately, luck intervened and Mlekush made a connection with Stonecipher, who was working at Life of Georgia at the time.

"Georgia US Corporation, which owned Life of Georgia, was in the process of acquiring Southland Life, and they wanted to relocate Southland to Atlanta, and they needed somebody to run it," Mlekush said. "This allowed me an opportunity to work for someone I had greatly admired. Then when David joined Jefferson-Pilot, he essentially brought me with him."[5]

Other executives soon followed. Dennis Glass joined in October 1993 as chief financial officer and executive vice president after a career at Northwestern Mutual Life and various other companies. He was recruited by Stonecipher and Hopkins.

E. Jay Yelton, Ph.D., signed on that same month. Yelton, executive vice president-investments, had previously served as director of the Florida State Treasury and chief economist for the state of Florida. At Jefferson-Pilot, he assumed responsibility for the company's investment portfolio.

In 1994, Hoyt Phillips joined as senior vice president-human resources, and Mark Konen was hired as senior vice president and corporate actuary to work in mergers and acquisitions.

Together, this group would shake up Jefferson-Pilot's culture so completely that most company veterans think of Jefferson-Pilot in terms of "before

Ken Mlekush joined Jefferson-Pilot as Executive Vice President in January 1993 as David Stonecipher's first hire. He moved quickly to revitalize the company's distribution network.

Stonecipher" and "the Stonecipher era." Before Stonecipher arrived, virtually everybody in the home office still identified themselves as a "Jefferson Standard" or a "Pilot" employee.

"It was steeped in its tradition," Phillips remembered of the company. "Compared to other cultures I've been in, it was a lot less political, a lot less bureaucratic, but it also didn't have the sense of urgency of some other companies."[6]

The new leadership would spread a sense of urgency throughout Jefferson-Pilot, introducing new policies and thought processes. It was actually to their advantage that none were insiders and only knew the company from what they had heard and observed as outsiders.

"We viewed Jefferson-Pilot as a career agency company in the southeastern part of the United States that was not a significant player from a marketing and distribution point of view," Mlekush remembered. "On the other hand, it had a great reputation, and I had high regard for everyone I knew from the company. It also had a great reputation for being extremely financially strong, and I felt it had all the key strengths to build a very strong national company. There were literally no skeletons in the closet. No negatives holding us back."[7]

Perhaps even better, Stonecipher and his management team discovered a healthy organization that welcomed change. In 1993, many employees felt that Jefferson-Pilot was poised to make a decision about what it would become in the future, and many of the dedicated core of loyalists were anxious for growth.

"Obviously, when David arrived, the culture was going to change," said John Ingram, a senior vice president-investments both before and after Stonecipher joined the company. "It's marvelous that we have had the opportunities to bring in new people with different backgrounds and experiences. Their contributions have given us tremendous insight as we have grown so dramatically over the last ten years."[8]

The IMO Channel

The first order of business within Stonecipher's two-part strategy was reorienting the way Jefferson-Pilot marketed and distributed its products. For 90 years, Jefferson-Pilot had relied on career agents operating from offices primarily in the Southeast. It was a successful strategy that had channeled billions of dollars of life insurance to people throughout the South.

By the mid-1990s, however, it was not feasible to dramatically expand the ranks of the company's career agents. Instead, the Stonecipher team began to recruit independent, third-party insurance agents and marketing firms all over the country to market Jefferson-Pilot products. Thus the Independent Marketing Organization channel, or IMO, was born. It was the first of several radical departures for a company that had previously been known as a "career agency company" that relied almost exclusively on career agents.

"Certainly," Stonecipher said, "the most essential change has been the reorientation of Jefferson-Pilot as an aggressive organization—a company on the move, particularly from a marketing perspective."[9]

Beginning on June 1, 1993, 30 IMOs were soon appointed, contracts signed, and procedures established. "At year end," Stonecipher said, "these individuals had under contract more than 3,400 agents and were telling the Jefferson-Pilot story in 46 states." That year, fourth-quarter sales tripled first-quarter sales.

Bill Pickering, a veteran field manager who joined Jefferson-Pilot in 1993, quickly distinguished his organization as the leading independent marketing organization. "Beginning in the early 1990s, career shops had captive agents," he said. "But one company cannot be everything to everybody. When the IMO people had the freedom to continue relationships possibly with other carriers and expand to a highly rated, extremely strong company like Jefferson-Pilot, it just exploded their growth unbelievably."[10]

The Career Agency Channel

At the same time it was building an IMO network, Jefferson-Pilot focused on improving its career agency operation. In 1993, there were 52 career agencies nationwide, many of them located in small towns throughout the Southeast. The company began by closing inefficient agencies or consolidating them with larger agencies. Within a few years, Jefferson-Pilot had just over 20 career agencies.

As the number of agencies was pared down, new management was recruited to run the division. Bill Seawell II, senior vice president-marketing, joined the home office in 1993 to help build the career agency channel. The son of Bill Seawell Jr.—who had served as a senior marketing officer for Jefferson Standard—Bill II was raised on Jefferson Road and rose through the career agency operation. Together with Roger Seigler, he had managed the Greensboro agency office through the 1980s. This was the same agency managed by W. H. Andrews Jr., a legendary insurance salesman and namesake of the W. H. Andrews Jr. Award.

Like Seawell, many of the ABGA agents had thrived within the Jefferson-Pilot family for decades. In Chapel Hill, Bill White—son of former Pilot President Rufus White—continued to serve as a successful Jefferson-Pilot producer. In Greensboro, Roger Seigler—son of Senior Vice President Ralph Seigler—continued to run the agency office.

"The primary challenge facing us as we entered 1993 was to restore sales momentum to all of Jefferson-Pilot's individual insurance marketing channels, particularly our key career agency system," Stonecipher later said. "We approached that challenge from two directions. First, we focused on how to utilize the company's existing major distribution systems more effectively, and, second, we looked at how we could expand distribution beyond our existing channels."[11]

Sharpening the Business

Increasing sales was one part of the challenge before Jefferson-Pilot. The company also looked for ways to maximize its existing businesses, reaching for leadership in its chosen markets and divesting operations that diluted the company's focus.

"To get to where we wanted to go would require great focus," Mlekush said. "Toward that end, David and the rest of us worked hard getting out of businesses that didn't contribute to where we wanted to go."[12]

In the early and mid-1990s, Jefferson-Pilot moved out of a number of older businesses that didn't fit with the plan. These divestitures included a property and casualty company, a title insurance company, and Pilot's group health department. This area in particular had continued to erode over the

years as the cost of health care rose relentlessly and consumers balked at paying the high premiums of group health coverage. In fact, Jefferson-Pilot was among many insurance companies that withdrew from group health insurance in the 1990s.

Pilot's home service operation was also restructured. Still under the management of Bob Martin, the home service line was "downsized, and we improved the productivity and profitability," Martin said. "A new middle-income marketing strategy was adopted, and once again the name was changed, this time to District Agency Network (DAN)."[13]

As these developments were unfolding, financial details from the 1993 annual report confirmed that Jefferson-Pilot's new strategies were working. In 1993, assets stood at $5.64 billion, shareholders' equity at $1.73 billion, and net income at $219.3 million. It was the company's strongest year on record. On February 14, 1994, the board increased cash dividends from 39 cents per share to 43 cents.

In 1994, Stonecipher's letter to shareholders noted that "career agency life sales were up almost 12 percent." In addition, the emerging IMO system had tripled its sales. "Against a background of declining industry sales," said an industry report, "Jefferson-Pilot achieved record life insurance sales, with total first-year premiums up over 49 percent."[14] That year, assets rose to $6.1 billion, and net income at $239.2 million, a rise of nearly 13 percent.

The First Acquisition

Meanwhile, the executive team at Jefferson-Pilot continued to look for acquisition possibilities, eager to put into motion the second part of Stonecipher's plan.

"We had our list of candidates that we were watching, and part of it was keeping abreast of what strategically was going on in their companies," remembered Mark Konen, executive vice president, product/financial management.[15]

Opposite: With its mix of products and services, Jefferson-Pilot attracted 3,400 independent agents within a year of founding the IMO channel. These agents soon accounted for more than 90 percent of sales.

If you're thinking about how many policies you can sell him, we wish you luck. If you're thinking about what you can do for him, we wish you were on our team.

You know the first type. For that agent, every encounter is a chance to move a lot of product. But in Jefferson Pilot Financial's long experience as a provider, we've had better relationships with agents who want just that with their customers—better relationships.

The kind built on a deep understanding of the customers' needs, as well as a thorough knowledge of what's available to meet those needs. And we've found out something interesting about the agents who trouble to gain this kind of relationship—they end up better off in the long run.

Perhaps it's because they see this industry in the way we do—as something more than simply selling insurance policies and other financial products. By helping our clients manage their money better, we are helping each of them gain control over their future. Or, as we have been known to say, we are helping them write the stories of their lives.

It's a bigger job when you look at it that way. And when it's done right, it comes with bigger rewards.

JEFFERSON PILOT
FINANCIAL

Helping you write the story of your life.℠

www.jpfinancial.com
Jefferson-Pilot Life Insurance Company and Jefferson Pilot Financial Insurance Company.
© 1999 Jefferson-Pilot Corporation. All Rights Reserved.
*Membership Promotes Ethical Market Conduct for Individual Life Insurance and Annuities.

In photo at left, Rosalyn and Jimmy Carter, third and fourth from right, pose with a Habitat for Humanity family and helpers. The Jefferson-Pilot crew gathers on the steps of a new home, photo at right. Also active in Greensboro, these pictures were taken during a Habitat building blitz in Kentucky, where employees from Jefferson-Pilot's Greensboro and Lexington, Kentucky, offices worked together to build a home.

The search required a special degree of tact because of the sensitive nature of the insurance industry. Acquiring life insurance companies are not buying machinery or patents or factories. Rather, they are buying people, intangible assets, and reputations. Hostile takeovers are almost unheard of in the life insurance business. Jefferson-Pilot needed to find companies that were willing to sell for one reason or another and would simultaneously provide an important strategic fit.

"We were always looking for things that would fit better with Jefferson-Pilot than they currently fit with whatever corporate entity they were involved with," Konen said. "Our strategic game plan was to look at acquisitions to augment our core business. Another key was the distribution outlets an acquisition might bring because we're always looking for increased distribution."[16]

In 1995, the first acquisition was unveiled when Jefferson-Pilot announced the $225 million acquisition of a block of policies of Kentucky Central Life based in Lexington, Kentucky. Although it did not bring added distribution, this acquisition showcased the talents of the new management team.

"This was a very well-executed transaction that even today continues to provide very good returns," Dennis Glass later said. "Although not as broadly strategic as later transactions, it was the first demonstration of the team's ability to creatively and successfully execute a purchase."[17]

Kentucky Central was an ideal candidate for Jefferson-Pilot's first purchase. The company had recently been seized by the Kentucky Insurance Department, which was looking for a way to protect the company's policy holders and the state guaranty funds that protect policy holders of insolvent companies. The Department supported Jefferson-Pilot's bid and submitted a plan to the Kentucky court system under which Jefferson-Pilot would assume most of Kentucky Central's life insurance and annuity business.

"We moved immediately and aggressively to build a framework for the rehabilitation of that company's life business which would both protect the approximately 400,000 Kentucky Central policy holders and provide new growth opportunities for Jefferson-Pilot," Stonecipher reported to Jefferson-Pilot shareholders.[18]

Stonecipher assured former Kentucky Central policy holders they were joining "our family of nearly 1.5 million policy holders. We care about you and your needs and we value your trust."

Alexander Hamilton Life

The year wouldn't even be out before Jefferson-Pilot announced its next acquisition. This time, Jefferson-Pilot successfully bid on Alexander Hamilton Life Insurance Company of America and First Alexander Hamilton Life Insurance Company from Household International.[19]

The purchase price of $575 million included $475 million in cash, $50 million in Alexander Hamilton Life stock, and the purchase from Household of a $50 million surplus note of Alexander Hamilton Life. In exchange, Jefferson-Pilot picked up an important distribution network in the Midwest.[20]

Although some joked that Alexander Hamilton was acquired because it "was first on the alphabetical list" of targets, the acquisition actually presented a more challenging situation. Jefferson-Pilot was one of at least seven bidders for the company, and it required some careful negotiating on David Stonecipher's part to land the deal.

"He did a masterful job of making the decision-makers on the other side of the table feel comfortable with us as a company going forward," Mlekush said. "He always spends a lot of time talking to his counterpart on the other side of the table about our culture and about our management philosophies and about how the company would fit with us."[21]

Fortunately, the fit was nearly perfect, both from a revenue and a strategic point of view. The companies had similar product lines in universal life and annuities, little overlap among the distribution channels, and complementary annuity markets. While Jefferson-Pilot was located primarily in the South, Alexander Hamilton was primarily midwestern, with a large presence in California, Florida, Michigan, New Jersey, Ohio, and Pennsylvania.

"Alexander Hamilton not only enhanced our independent distribution platform, it also got us into geographical areas that we had no exposure to before, primarily the Midwestern part of the United States," Mlekush said. "It also improved our annuity offerings by a substantial amount."[22]

The most delicate issue surrounding the acquisition was the relocation of Alexander Hamilton's operations to North Carolina. As with any acquisition-related relocation, it was a difficult process. In the end, the relocation was accomplished as smoothly as possible, and the newly combined organization began to reap the benefits of its consolidation.

The Chubb Life Acquisition

With two acquisitions already completed, Jefferson-Pilot management still wasn't satisfied. Just over a year after closing the Alexander Hamilton acquisition, Jefferson-Pilot made its next strategic move. This time it would bite off a larger chunk with even further-reaching implications. On February 23, 1997, Jefferson-Pilot acquired all the outstanding shares of Chubb Life Insurance Company of America for $875 million. The move doubled Jefferson-Pilot's life insurance business, added a major new distribution channel, the General Agency, or GA channel, and was strategically critical for the future.

"In the long term, Chubb Life's unique position in the upper markets—particularly in variable universal life sales—will be a significant marketing advantage," Stonecipher said at the time. "We will become a major force in variable universal life (VUL). By the same token, Jefferson-Pilot has strong universal life and survivorship insurance products that will be valuable to Chubb Life's producers."[23]

Stonecipher's focus on VUL was an indication of how important that market had become. By the late 1990s, VUL had built on the success of universal life insurance to become the fastest growing and most important kind of life insurance in the market. Through Chubb, Jefferson-Pilot had purchased a strong position.

"Chubb Life was significant because it took Jefferson-Pilot into variable products," said John Hopkins, general counsel, who had once again managed the legal side of the acquisition. "Jefferson-Pilot was not a significant writer of variable products, and Chubb Life had a very good variable life insurance operation. It also had a larger and more sophisticated broker dealer operation."[24]

Chubb Life's location in New Hampshire raised the obvious question of relocation. Naturally, many Chubb Life employees were worried about being uprooted, a concern that had plagued employees throughout the auction process, even before Jefferson-Pilot became involved. "There were a lot of issues and uncertainty," remembered Ron Angarella, then president of Chubb Life's broker dealer and later senior vice president, General Agency, for Jefferson Pilot Financial and chairman and CEO of Jefferson Pilot Securities Corporation. "Then once we knew that Jefferson-Pilot was going to be the acquiring company, people felt pretty good about it because of the strategic fit organizationally."[25]

With the previous acquisitions, the relocation issue had been relatively easy to handle. Kentucky Central Life and Alexander Hamilton were consolidated over time into the company's Greensboro operations. Chubb Life, however, presented more difficult integration planning issues: Its variable operation was central to Jefferson-Pilot's future strategy, and Jefferson-Pilot had no significant variable capability in Greensboro. Moreover, Chubb Life's highly talented workforce was deeply rooted in New Hampshire. Fortunately, Stonecipher had foreseen this conflict, and the acquisition planning included the decision that the Chubb Life offices in New Hampshire would remain open.

"We made the decision before the deal was done that we weren't going to fully integrate it into Greensboro because it would have caused us to add a substantial number of people," Mlekush said. "We also knew a lot of their people weren't going to be willing to relocate to Greensboro, North Carolina, because they were lifelong residents of New Hampshire."[26]

The Chubb Life people turned out to be one of the major benefits of the acquisition. Chubb Life's top producers had an immediate impact on Jefferson-Pilot's sales, and many of the company's officers moved to Jefferson-Pilot. These included Terry Stone, first as president of Jefferson-Pilot Communications and later chief financial officer of Jefferson-Pilot Corporation; Chuck Cornelio as executive vice president of underwriting-new business and chief information officer; Angarella; and leaders in human resources and administrative services. It was refreshing for these Chubb executives to find themselves part of a company that valued VUL so highly.

"In the mid-1990s, I was invited to become president of Chubb's life insurance business because there were some very strategic issues that needed to be addressed," remembered Stone. "At Chubb Life, we determined that we should really concentrate all of our resources on the life insurance business. Jefferson-Pilot ended up approaching Chubb Corporation about buying the life insurance businesses, knowing that it was the smaller of that corporation's two business, but it was the core business for Jefferson-Pilot. So it was a good fit."[27]

Ultimately, said Angarella, the merger represented forward motion for both companies.

"As an independent entity, Chubb Life brought to the table the largest individual insurance distribution organization within Jefferson-Pilot Corporation," he said. "Equally important, Chubb Life brought a focus on high-end markets, particularly in VUL sales, which is essential in today's market. Combined with the other life distribution channels, we have a company which can successfully compete in a landscape increasingly dominated by industry giants."[28]

Just after the merger, the Chubb Life and Jefferson-Pilot broker dealers were combined to create Jefferson Pilot Securities Corporation (JPSC). Through JPSC, 2,400 registered representatives sold a wide range of securities products, including variable universal life. Between 1997 and 2000, JPSC grew 30 percent annually.

"The biggest benefit that fueled the growth during that time was that we were able to take the more mature securities platform Chubb had and introduce that into the Jefferson-Pilot channels," Angarella said. "In a three-year period, we doubled the securities sales because of the service, support, education, training, and the overall platform we could provide."[29]

From a cultural point of view, the acquisition was a success almost immediately. Because of the decision to sustain and enhance the Concord operation, there was little cultural friction between people from New Hampshire and people from North Carolina.

"By and large, they shared common goals and objectives: success for the company; success for the project they were working on; and success in finding ways to do things smarter and more efficiently," Cornelio said. "Jefferson-Pilot is a very efficient company. It's very conscious of its expenses and how efficiently it can deliver product, and that became a real guiding principle for the people who came from Chubb. The Jefferson-Pilot people learned that it's okay to present outside-the-box thoughts to people, that it was all right to stick your head up above the horizon and say, 'How about we do this even if it's a radical idea?' "[30]

The Communications Story

Jefferson-Pilot Communications grew alongside the life insurance business, yet the middle 1990s were poignant years. In 1995, Joseph M. Bryan passed away. Bryan, the son-in-law of Julian Price, and a longtime board member, had founded Jefferson-Pilot Communications through the oppor-

Chubb Life headquarters in Concord, New Hampshire. Chubb Life Insurance was the smaller sibling of Chubb Property & Casualty, but it was a leader in the important variable universal life insurance market.

tunistic purchase of WBIG in Greensboro. He had run the company for the next several decades as it expanded into television and sports productions. In his final years, even after retiring from the board of directors, he maintained an office in Jefferson-Pilot's headquarters.

Although his absence was felt, he had long ago ceded his operational role at Jefferson-Pilot Communications. William E. "Bill" Blackwell, long-time executive of the Jefferson-Pilot Corporation, was named senior vice president and director of JP Broadcasting in 1984. Then, in 1991, he was named president of Jefferson-Pilot Communications. During his leadership, the company grew substantially, including adding two more radio signals in

San Diego, an FM signal in Charlotte, and a fourth signal in Denver, as well as a television station in Charleston, South Carolina.

The company now owned radio stations in Atlanta, Charlotte, Denver, Miami, and San Diego, and television stations in Charlotte, Richmond and Charleston. In all, it had about 1,000 employees. The television stations fell under the purview of John Shreves, president of the television division, and the radio division was managed by Clarke Brown.[31]

In 1997, Blackwell announced his retirement, and Terry Stone was tapped to fill the top role at Jefferson-Pilot Communications. Stone promised that Jefferson-Pilot Communications would continue to grow through smart acquisitions.

Interestingly, although Jefferson-Pilot Communications was much smaller than the insurance operations, it was the most visible part of the company. In the mid-1990s, Jefferson-Pilot conducted one of its occasional studies on name recognition and found that most people, especially in the Southeast, recognized the company as a communications and media firm.

This was not necessarily a bad thing. From its earliest days, Jefferson-Pilot Communications had sought to raise awareness of the parent corporation through advertising, media ownership, and sports sponsorships managed by Jefferson-Pilot Sports. Its widespread name recognition and status as the premier midsize media company was a measure of how successful it had been in spreading the Jefferson-Pilot name.

"It's been an exciting, challenging path," said Ed Hull, president of Jefferson-Pilot Sports. "It's been an opportunity to get the name out as the company has grown more national in perspective."[32]

One of the most memorable experiences for Jefferson-Pilot Sports occurred in 1996 in conjunction with the Summer Olympic Games. Four years earlier, Jefferson-Pilot Sports had already created a syndicated gymnastics show, using the same model it followed for figure skating championships. In 1996, Jefferson-Pilot Sports did it once again, this time creating three television shows around the American gymnastics team and taking the team on a 48-state tour called the Kodak Road to Olympic Gold, hosted by Mary Lou Retton and broadcaster Pat O'Brien.

This show led to one of the most touching events in Hull's career. Just before the Olympics got underway, Jefferson-Pilot Sports brought the team to Greensboro for final training before going to Atlanta. "Obviously, it's a closed training venue," Hull remembered. "There was no publicity around it, and we had the team in Greensboro for two weeks. The city of Greensboro supported them 100 percent, and as a result, they put on a private show. During the show, we surprised the girls by bringing Mary Lou Retton into their practice. She was the role model for the girls, and we let her come and give a very heartwarming speech to the girls."[33]

Terry Stone, formerly with Chubb Life, joined Jefferson-Pilot as President of Jefferson-Pilot Communications after the acquisition. In late 2002, she was named Chief Financial Officer of Jefferson-Pilot Corporation.

Before the 1996 U.S. Women's Gymnastics Team brought home Olympic Gold, Jefferson-Pilot Sports brought the team to Greensboro, North Carolina, for a last round of training. The team members, dressed in matching outfits, attended a luncheon hosted by Jefferson-Pilot at the City Club located at the top of the Jefferson-Pilot Building.

This team went on to capture the team gold medal for the United States after a dramatic individual vault by the injured Kerri Strug.

Guarantee Life Companies

In the years surrounding the Olympics, Jefferson-Pilot pulled off an award-winning performance of its own: Between 1995 and 1997, the company successfully assimilated three major acquisitions. In 1998, in an effort to unite the fast-moving pieces, Jefferson-Pilot unveiled a new corporate logo.

"With the release of these corporate identity standards, we have created the foundation for a powerful, consistent image for all communications pieces," Stonecipher announced. "In our logo, and its associated brand identity, you see the image of a class company—the class of market leadership, financial quality, professional employees, and shareholder performance."[34]

It wasn't long after the logo was introduced that executives announced a fourth major acquisition. This purchase, unveiled on December 30, 1999, would affect one of the company's oldest business groups.

At the time, Jefferson-Pilot still had a fairly substantial group life and disability operation although there was speculation the group operation would soon be divested. Throughout the 1990s, various consultants had been hired to revamp the group business and give it a sense of strategy.

"When we were trying to figure out what we were going to do with the group, we had a lot of different consultants and people brought in to help us," said Ann Dowd, an account manager who had worked in Pilot's group division since the 1950s. "We were constantly changing to match what they felt, which was good. We were getting used to the idea that you must have change to grow."[35]

Jefferson-Pilot put any speculation to rest when it announced the acquisition in 1998 of the Guarantee Life Companies of Omaha, Nebraska, for $425 million, including cash and assumption of debt. Guarantee Life had a large group operation and a smaller individual life insurance unit. The company offered individual life insurance, ancillary (nonmedical) group and worksite insurance products, including life, long-term and short-term disability, and dental through a nationwide distribution system consisting of regional sales offices in addition to the home office in Omaha.

Jefferson-Pilot announced it would combine its group operation with Guarantee's group business in Omaha under the management of Bob Bates, chairman and CEO of Guarantee Life and a national leader in group life and disability. The new group division would be renamed the Benefit Partners business unit and represented about 10 percent of Jefferson-Pilot's earnings. Meanwhile, Guarantee's individual life insurance business was relocated to Greensboro.

Interestingly, Bates said, Guarantee's group business was actually much younger than Jefferson-Pilot's. Guarantee, which was founded in 1901, had only been in the ancillary group benefits business since the early 1990s. A mutual company for 95 years, Guarantee demutualized in 1995, becoming a publicly traded company.

"When I joined Guarantee in 1989, we evaluated the opportunities within the industry and went into the ancillary group benefits business with a rather counter-intuitive notion that a new player without the baggage of the past could actually create competitive advantage against some very formidable and sizable competitors," Bates said. "That's turned out to be true. We have the ability to move rapidly. We have developed cutting edge technology. We put our arrangements together with Jefferson-Pilot after

concluding that our best chance to capitalize on what we built was to affiliate with a larger company."[36]

In fact, Bates said, Guarantee initiated the acquisition. "We targeted several companies based on my knowledge of their chief executives," Bates said. "We also targeted companies that were in the group insurance business and we thought might have an interest in continuing in that business, and if they did, would see an enormous value that we could bring to their company. It was a foregone conclusion in my mind that everybody would consolidate our individual business into theirs."[37]

The acquisition was an excellent example of Jefferson-Pilot's willingness to borrow ideas from

Bob Bates, Chairman and CEO of Guarantee Life in Omaha, Nebraska, continued to run the company after Jefferson-Pilot acquired it in 1999. Guarantee had one of the most successful group operations in the country.

the companies it acquired. "When it was purchased by Jefferson-Pilot, Guarantee Life had a casual dress policy, with five casual days a week, while Jefferson-Pilot had a more formal dress code," said Hoyt Phillips. "We made the decision to modify our dress policy to business casual five days a week across the corporation."[38]

Not only would Jefferson-Pilot change its dress code, it also recognized the success of Guarantee's existing technology platform.

"We brought leading-edge technology," Bates said. "We brought great talent, and we brought a commitment to training and maximizing that talent. Jefferson-Pilot recognized the value of this commitment and used it to strengthen its performance-based culture."[39]

Guarantee Life Companies' headquarters in Omaha, Nebraska. Purchased in 1999, Guarantee, since merged into Jefferson Pilot Financial Insurance Company, became headquarters for the Benefit Partners group insurance business unit.

This assessment was shared by leaders at Jefferson-Pilot. "They had technology," Mlekush said. "They had a staff of people we were very impressed with, and the result was that we integrated all of the Jefferson-Pilot group life and disability operation into Guarantee Life."[40]

With Guarantee Life Companies' assets of nearly $2 billion, Jefferson-Pilot counted consolidated assets of more than $26 billion. And the new business generated was "expected to exceed $400 million in annual premiums and equivalents."[41]

The Growth Effect

The net effect of these acquisitions was exhilarating. By the end of 2000, sales of life insurance at Jefferson-Pilot were six times greater than they had been in 1992.[42] The corporation's stock was trading at $75.88 per share, approximately double its average price four years earlier. Life insurance in force was at $218.5 billion, more than double the value of four years earlier. Assets exceeded $27.3 billion.

It was time, Stonecipher decided, to revisit Jefferson-Pilot's strategic direction. Stonecipher retained the consulting firm McKinsey & Company to return to Jefferson-Pilot and assess the future. Together with senior Jefferson-Pilot executives, the consulting team mapped out a new strategy and financial goals. They agreed it was time for Jefferson-Pilot to focus on organic and organizational growth and pull away from large acquisitions.

In the future, Jefferson-Pilot would be a marketing-driven organization rather than a product-driven organization. It would focus on wealth preservation, wealth accumulation, and business planning for its customers, offering a more comprehensive platform of products and services.

After seven years of remarkable growth, this was a perfectly logical roadmap into the future. Jefferson-Pilot had more opportunities than ever before to reach consumers, with such distribution channels as the IMO, the GA channel, JPSC and the career agency channel. In 2001, the career agency channel was renamed the Agency Building General Agent system, or ABGA.

Eager to maximize the strength of Jefferson-Pilot's marketing organization, management created a series of new products and goals to knit together Jefferson-Pilot's portfolio. The Vision series, for example, bound a portfolio of universal life products. The company also increased the target production levels for agents, which increased life policy applications per agent by 28 percent and increased annualized life premiums per agent by 25 percent. Finally, a new recruiting system was created and a new compensation package was introduced to better reward the most productive agents.

Still, management was looking for new ways to drive sales. "We were very successful," Stonecipher later said. "However, times changed, and we knew that, without making significant changes, our growth curve would remain the same as everyone else.... While some companies might be content with this, we did not believe it was an acceptable attitude for a true market leader. So our challenge became, how do we get back on a dramatic growth curve?"[43]

The answer presented itself in a new program: the Premier Partner program, originally introduced in 1999. First under the management of Ken Mlekush, the Premier Partners program rewarded top-producing agents with increased access to the home office and administrative support. It was rapidly accepted and quickly successful.

In 2000, Jefferson-Pilot introduced the Premier Partnering Strategy as a way to drive sales. There were two key goals: double the number of Premier Partners, and increase life insurance sales by 50 percent.

Pleased with the program's success, in 2000 Jefferson-Pilot announced the Premier Partnering Strategy and unveiled new, ambitious goals: By the end of 2002, the company would increase life sales by 50 percent, a significant achievement in an industry that was reporting flat sales, and double the number of Premier Partners managers and producers to more than 500.

Broadcasting Excellence

These goals—already audacious—would soon take on added significance. In early 2000, shortly after the election of George W. Bush as president, the United States slipped into a brief recession. While the insurance operation continued to grow, the weight of the recession fell for a short time on Jefferson-Pilot Communications as the advertising industry fell into its deepest slump in a decade.

Fortunately, the downturn ended quickly, and the economy staggered through an uneven recovery in 2000 and 2001. The recovery, however, was savagely interrupted on September 11, 2001, when terrorist attacks destroyed the World Trade Center in New York City and crashed planes into the Pentagon and rural Pennsylvania. In the months after the attacks, the economy virtually ground to a halt.

Although impacted for a brief period, Jefferson-Pilot Communications soon regained its strong performance. With three network television stations in Charlotte, North Carolina, Richmond, Virginia, and Charleston, South Carolina, and 17 radio stations in Atlanta, Charlotte, Denver, Miami, and San Diego, and Jefferson-Pilot Sports, its sports production and syndication business, Jefferson-Pilot Communications had gained wide respect as the premier midsize communications business in the country.

"Because of our great TV and radio markets," said Terry Stone, president of Jefferson-Pilot Communications, "we have continued to experience excellent growth. In our radio, television, and sports businesses, our teams have a very strong sense of ownership and urgency and are required to be on their toes competitively every day. Feedback is quick and constant—we are competing in the market every day. And the scorecards on audience ratings performance and advertising market share are available on an ongoing basis.

"Everyone at our stations—the team might be 50 to 200 people at a location—is focused on success in the marketplace and delivering the bottom line. They are competitive people who want to win. At our 17 radio stations in top-50 markets, three television stations, and our successful sports broadcasting business, the professionals who guided Jefferson-Pilot Communications through the period so well did so because they share a commitment to quality, trust, and reliability, which are the cornerstones of the entire Jefferson-Pilot culture."[44]

As Jefferson-Pilot approached its 100th anniversary, the communications business promised continued success and growth. From its humble beginning with its first radio station in 1934 to its status among the elite broadcast companies of its size, Jefferson-Pilot Communications has exhibited broadcasting excellence for decades.

The Number One Spot

While the recession obviously affected every business in America, the insurance operations of Jefferson-Pilot seemed to defy gravity. On July 10, 2002—just over a year into the Premier Partnering Strategy—a memo was released to home-office employees declaring "WE'RE NO. 1!"

The memo announced Jefferson-Pilot had topped the industry in fixed universal life insurance sales: "Jefferson Pilot Financial topped the industry in fixed universal life sales in the first quarter of 2002, according to a survey by LIMRA International. JPF moved from 4th, at the end of 2001, to the No. 1 spot, the first time the company had reached that position. JPF also for the first time moved into the top 10 in total life sales, moving from 14th to 10th, according to LIMRA."[45]

This achievement was no accident of timing. It called to mind remarks of the management team made a decade earlier.

"We told them right out of the box that we were going to double sales in five years," Stonecipher said, "and their eyes would glaze over. But we doubled sales in three years rather than five. If you can have successes, it builds excitement, and it builds belief in the culture. Slowly but surely I think we've done that."[46]

Going forward, Stonecipher said, Jefferson-Pilot would stick with the strategy that had served

PREMIER PARTNERS

THE PREMIER PARTNER PROGRAM WAS introduced in 1999 and proved highly successful. In 2000, the successful program was expanded into the Premier Partnering Strategy, which had an ambitious goal: Double the number of Premier Partners to 500 and increase life sales by 50 percent by year-end 2002.

Like most insurance companies, Jefferson-Pilot realized about 80 percent of its sales from about 20 percent of its agents. The company had about 18,000 active agents, of which only 240 were Premier Partners. By 2003, Jefferson-Pilot hoped to have 500 Premier Partners. These Premier Partners helped increase the company's life insurance sales by 60 percent in two years.

There were good reasons for an agent to aspire to Premier Partner status. Premier Partners received a superior level of home office support, could set their sights on spectacular incentive trips, and generally enjoyed better service. These extras included a dedicated underwriter and service support people at the home office. Each Premier Partner was also assigned a company ambassador to help with issues or talk about the general direction of the company.

"Our most recent challenge has been the implementation of the Premier Partnering Strategy," said Stonecipher in late 2002. "It has been the most rapid culture change I've ever experienced. We're putting our time and attention into those who are giving us business."[1]

By 2003, through the General Agency (GA) and Independent Marketing distribution channels, Jefferson-Pilot derived about 90 percent of its sales from independent agents who ran their own businesses, free to offer products from any company. In most cases, independent agents strived to create the right mix of products.

"The lifeblood of an agent is the relationships he or she establishes with clients, his management team, the home office, and the underwriting and policy holder service," said career agent and Premier Partner Sam Cornwell. "When Jefferson-Pilot made the decision to emphasize Premier Partners, it showed a great respect for those who work hard and produce."[2]

Ron Agel, a Premier Partner in the GA channel, agreed that relationships are key to the business. "I've never found that people buy product," Agel said. "I've always found that people buy the agent. They buy quality, and they look to me to be their point man to find quality in the marketplace. Jefferson-Pilot is a quality company."[3]

Like many Premier Partners, Agel had previously represented one of the acquired companies, Chubb Life, which was well represented among the ranks of Premier Partners. Jefferson-Pilot was eager to retain as many top Chubb Life agents as possible; Guy Hatcher was among them.

"You could see the vision of Jefferson-Pilot very soon after the acquisition, and new things were introduced, including the Premier Partner program," Hatcher said.[4]

A large number of veteran IMO producers and managers were included in the ranks of Jefferson-Pilot Premier Partners. Bill Pickering, manager of the company's leading independent marketing organization, gave some reasons the company was attractive to successful independent producers. "The thing that has made Jefferson-Pilot a leader is they don't play games in the pricing of products," Pickering said. "Jefferson-Pilot's strategic long-term position is to maintain high financial ratings in the industry so the larger client will feel safe in doing business with a company that has the integrity Jefferson-Pilot has."[5]

Part of the program's success must be credited to Jefferson-Pilot's commitment. The insurance industry has long relied on incentives, but Premier Partners set itself apart because it represented a strategic redirection for Jefferson-Pilot.

"I think the company is really quite innovative," said Premier Partner Dave Misiak. "Once you reach Premier Partner status, you have special lines to call to get underwriting information, commission information, or policy service. You get things done for you more quickly."[6]

The program also included the Premier Partners Advisory Counsel, which offered an opportunity for senior management to huddle with top agents in product development sessions. Michael Lyman, a Premier Partner and former member of the Advisory Counsel, worked on the committee that recommended keeping Ensemble II in the company's product portfolio.

"Product shelf life is about three years; therefore it is important to be able to implement changes and modifications quickly," Lyman said. "I dedicate a large portion of my time, business and loyalty to Jefferson-Pilot because of the management team and their philosophy."[7]

Good products were matched by Jefferson-Pilot's speed to market. "I think one of the strengths of the company is that they're somewhat ahead of the curve in getting competitive products to the marketplace," said Premier Partner Norm Feinstein. "That's not always the case with an insurance company. Jefferson-Pilot has outstanding universal life products, which we represent almost exclusively."[8]

Even beyond marketing, the company's mission appealed to top producers. "I take care of widows and orphans," said J. J. Field. "I get letters from children, who write, 'J. J., I would never have gone to college if not for you.'"[9]

The subject of helping people invariably comes up among top producers. Premier Partners are excellent salespeople, not only because Jefferson-Pilot offers the right product mix and support services, but because they believe in their work. Loretta Courson, a Premier Partner and recipient of the prestigious W. H. Andrews Award in 2000, remarked, "I had so much fun selling life insurance.

"My clients are my best friends. I have gone through their marriages, children, and divorce," Courson said. "I had one client who called me with only weeks to live. I remember he looked at me in the hospital and said, 'Come sit on the bed here. Look me in the eye. I want you to be there for my wife because you're the only one I trust.'"[10]

Bernie Bernstein, another Premier Partner and winner of the 1997 W. H. Andrews award, says agents must believe in what they do. "Without life insurance, there would be a multitude of struggling widows, uneducated children, failed businesses, and retirees without money or dignity. Without life insurance, savings, tax-planning, and investments might amount to naught in the long run.

"No financial product is a substitute for life insurance. No financial product guarantees funds and liquidity at the very moment they are needed—at the time of death. Without life insurance, life is truly a gamble."[11]

The 2002 Sustaining Premier Partners in attendance at Jefferson-Pilot's annual Premier Partner Symposium. Sustaining Premier Partners qualified for the program for four consecutive years.

it so well. In 2002, the company announced several deals, including an alliance with Allstate.

The association with Allstate was one of a host of connections forged to put new products into even newer channels of distribution. Other alliances included a joint marketing initiative with Banc of America Investment Services to make Jefferson-Pilot's "Premier 5" annuity available to bank clients in 18 states and the District of Columbia,[47] and an arrangement with the Vanguard Group to sell a "Vanguard Single 5" fixed annuity, underwritten by Jefferson-Pilot, to tax-sensitive investors looking for a supplement to retirement savings plans.[48]

Through these alliances and its homegrown efforts, Jefferson-Pilot had increased its distribution channels from one in 1992 to seven in 2003.

At the same time, the company introduced a new advertising campaign. The new ads were designed "to separate Jefferson Pilot's message from the financial services advertising clutter."[49] The ads showed the kind of financial freedom that Jefferson-Pilot clients could enjoy.

Sales responded; the records set in mid-2002 were exceeded the very next quarter. "The second quarter and first six months represented the best quarterly and six-month life insurance sales performance in JPF's history," according to a company press release. "For the first six months, life insurance sales totaled nearly $132.6 million, 67.2 percent greater than the same period last year, and 15.3 percent higher than our previous six-month record performance."[50] In all, Jefferson-Pilot, including the offices in Concord, New Hampshire, and Greensboro, North Carolina, processed about 70,000 applications for insurance a year. Of these, about 15,000 needed special attention from a team of underwriters.

Since Stonecipher and his management team joined the company, Jefferson-Pilot had vaulted from number 64 in total life insurance sales in 1993 to number 11 in its industry at the end of 2002. It had helped lead the industry in a time of consoli-

Jefferson-Pilot's board of directors in 2003. From left, David A. Stonecipher, Chairman and CEO; Kenneth C. Mlekush, Vice Chairman of Jefferson-Pilot Corp. and President-Life Companies; E. S. "Jim" Melvin, President and CEO of The Joseph M. Bryan Foundation of Greater Greensboro; William H. Cunningham, Professor at the University of Texas at Austin; Patrick S. Pittard, former Chairman, President, and CEO of Heidrick & Struggles International; Robert G. Greer, Vice Chairman of Bank of Texas; Elizabeth Valk Long, former Executive Vice President of Time, Inc., and former President of *Time* magazine; William Porter Payne, Partner at Gleacher Partners LLC; George W. Henderson III, Chairman and CEO of Burlington Industries; Edwin B. Borden, President and CEO of the Borden Manufacturing Company; and Donald S. Russell Jr., an attorney in Columbia, South Carolina.

dation, compiling an incredible record of successful acquisitions. Amazingly, even six years into its acquisition program, Jefferson-Pilot executives were able to say that every single acquisition had worked.

"I always kid the folks on the financial side that the easy part of an acquisition is making it," Mlekush said. "The hard part is making it work after you get it. We've got a tremendous record in that regard."[51]

"The cultural aspects of acquisitions are the toughest," Stonecipher agreed. "But we've been the favored acquirer in a number of the acquisitions, and we've learned to identify and adopt best practices."[52]

Jefferson-Pilot had managed this organizational overhaul without major disruptions to its employees or traditions. Although there was some employee dislocation, it was negligible considering the magnitude of change, and the company maintained its integrity and ethical standards. It had smartly managed its growth—although some longtime veterans retained a wistfulness for the days of company parties and dances. Nevertheless, even the most nostalgic recognized that the core values that formed Jefferson Standard and Pilot Life had not changed.

"This is a corporation that, when you identify with it, you feel good," said Phillips. "You feel like you're working for an employer that is out for the good of everybody, the community, the employees, the shareholders."[53]

The theme that runs through Jefferson-Pilot's performance throughout the 1990s and the first years of the new millennium is that of a company realizing its potential. Stonecipher and his team unlocked the energy that had built up in Jefferson-Pilot like headwaters behind a dam.

"We tried to create a high-performance cultural ethic, and many of the people who were here when we came in 1993 were excited and wanted to be a part of it," Mlekush said. "They have grown very, very well with it."[54]

A Performance Culture

By late 2001, as the company neared its Premier Partner Strategy goals, new leadership began to move into position. Dennis Glass, president-financial operations and chief financial officer, was promoted to president and chief operating officer of Jefferson-Pilot Corporation. At the same time, Terry Stone, president of Jefferson-Pilot Communications, was tapped to become chief financial officer, and Ken Mlekush, president-life companies, was named vice chairman of Jefferson-Pilot's board of directors.

In October 2002, Warren May joined Jefferson-Pilot as executive vice president-marketing and distribution to lead the company's sales and marketing efforts. May came to Jefferson-Pilot from Travelers Life & Annuity, where he was chief executive officer

of Travelers Life Distributors. Like others who had joined the company over the last decade, May immediately noticed the sense of momentum and opportunity at Jefferson-Pilot.

"We have very disciplined, focused people," May said. "They are risk-takers who are not afraid to make the tough decisions that truly are right for our business."[55]

Glass, as the company's new president, helped to refine the strategic plan authored nearly a decade before. The Premier Partner strategy is a bold plan to capture the building process of the previous ten years and take the business to the next level.[56] Having the aggressive Premier Partner goals in mind, he recognized the need to reinvigorate the emphasis on people development and motivation as well as improve quality throughout the organization.

"The phrase 'performance culture' describes what it's about: performance—and creating a companywide culture that promotes aggressive goals and provides tools, training and job rotation to prepare employees to meet those goals," Glass said. "Basically, it is a culture in which every employee understands the organization's mission and priorities and their own agreed-upon goals to meet the stated mission."[57]

Indeed, elements of the performance culture could soon be seen throughout Jefferson-Pilot, as could the focus on quality and an effort called "lean manufacturing."

"Lean manufacturing is really process manufacturing," Glass said. "It is learning how to do the same job more effectively. In essence, it is a method for closely aligning processes in a function to optimize physical and human resources productivity."[58]

"It's an attempt to improve service and significantly improve the quality of our work, and therefore become more efficient," said Chuck Cornelio, chief information officer. The information systems function was especially challenging as Jefferson-Pilot tried simultaneously to offer more information over the Web and convert policies from the acquired companies to Jefferson-Pilot's system.[59]

By 2003, Jefferson-Pilot was a vastly changed organization. With new leadership moving into place, the company had undergone a cultural, geographical, and psychological transformation as profound as anything it had ever experienced. It had become a *Fortune* 500 company—making the list in 2003, 2002, and 2001—and a leader in its industry.

Yet some things would not change. The company's innate sense of integrity, reaching back to the very founding of the company, was intact. Jefferson-Pilot maintained its sense of pride, its roots in Greensboro, and its dedication to improving the lives of its insured. This sense of returning to the community and helping people had imbued Jefferson-Pilot with a strong ethical sense for 100 years. And it was reinforced almost daily through

Warren May joined Jefferson Pilot Financial as Executive Vice President-Marketing and Distribution in 2002. He was given responsibility for the company's sales and marketing efforts.

the hundreds of stories shared by agents who were able to deliver help to customers in a time of need.

Just one of these many stories was related by Dorothy Austell, a top-producing agent for Jefferson-Pilot since the 1950s and the first woman ever elected a trustee for two terms of the National Association of Life Underwriters.

"Our customers rely on you so much," she said. "One of my customers, a man and his wife, signed insurance with me when they were thirty years old. Then, on September 1, 2001, he got his walking papers. He was making $72,000 a year, and his wife was making $65,000. All of a sudden, he didn't have a job and he was 52 years old. They called and said, 'Come out and see us, Dorothy.' They told me their story, and they said, 'We want to thank you for what you did for us. We listened to you from the time we started up to now, and we have enough to take care of ourselves.' They put their arms around me and they kissed me on the cheek and said, 'God's going to bless you.' I said, 'He already has.'"[60]

To the employees of Jefferson-Pilot, these stories were a constant reminder of why they did what they did. The growth strategy at Jefferson-Pilot was not only designed to increase market share and benefit shareholders and executives. It also aimed to help the employees, communities, and families who depended on the company for financial security. Through their focus, David Stonecipher and the Jefferson-Pilot team built an enduring company that already looked forward to its next century.

"This company was built in the merger of several companies in the past," Stonecipher said in 2003. "When we go forward, certainly another 100 years, it's going to be an amalgamation of a lot more companies. If it's a growing, dynamic organization, we'll be just as relevant then as we are today."[61]

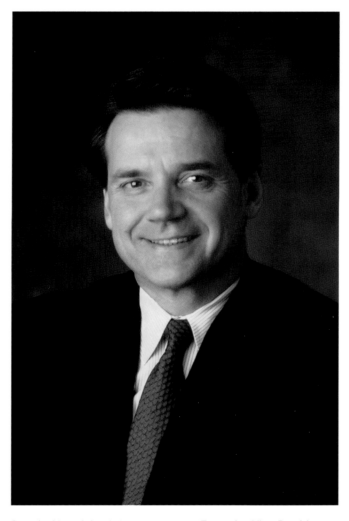

Dennis Glass joined the company as Executive Vice President and CFO. He led the merger and acquisition efforts along with key team members Mark Konen and John Hopkins, resulting in a series of transformative acquisitions between 1993 and 1999. In 2001, he was appointed President and Chief Operating Officer.

Notes to Sources

Chapter One

1. Mark Sullivan and Dan Rather, *In Our Times* (New York: Scribner, 1996), p. 36.
2. Ibid.
3. "The Stump Becomes an Oak," *State*, 12 December 1953, p. 3.
4. "Office Rules Pilot Life Insurance Co.", undated, Jefferson-Pilot archive.
5. "Stump Becomes an Oak."
6. "Special 75th Anniversary Tribute," 1 July 1978, Jefferson-Pilot archive.
7. "Office Rules Pilot Life Insurance Co.," undated, Jefferson-Pilot archive.
8. "Rotogravure Picture Section, Pilot Life Insurance Company," *Greensboro Daily Record*, 1928.
9. "Stump Becomes an Oak."
10. *The Pilot*, vol. 1, no. 1, January 1913, p. 1.
11. Ibid.
12. Ibid.
13. Ibid.
14. "75th anniversary: Pilot Life Insurance Marks Another Milestone," *Greensboro Daily News*, 25 June 1978, p. F-1.
15. "Stump Becomes an Oak."
16. Alexander W. McAlister Papers, 1886–1946; Collection Number 4318. UNC-Chapel Hill library, Manuscripts Department.
17. "Report on Our Free Examination," *The Pilot*, vol. 2, no. 6, June 1914, p. 1.
18. "Looking to the Future," *The Pilot*, vol. 5. no. 1, January 1917, p. 3.
19. "Annual Dividends in 1920," *The Pilot*, Vol. 7, No. 49, 16 December 1919, p. 1.
20. "A Thought for the New Year," *The Pilot*, Vol. 7, No. 51, 30 December 1919, p. 1.
21. Ethel Stevens Arnett, *Greensboro North Carolina* (University of North Carolina Press, 1955), p. 225.
22. P. D. Gold, "In the Beginning," *The Jeffersonian*, August 1957.
23. *Greensboro Daily News*, 19 November 1933, p. 8B.
24. P. D. Gold, "In the Beginning."
25. "The Jefferson Standard," *The State*, 11 August 1945, pp. 4–7
26. "ABC of Life Insurance," sales pamphlet (Spectator Company: New York), 1913.
27. Minutes of the board of directors, 1910. Jefferson-Pilot archive.
28. Arnett, *Greensboro North Carolina.*
29. "Greensboro Growth," *Greensbroo Daily News*, 29 May 1971, p. D2.
30. Arnett, *Greensboro North Carolina.*
31. Jack Scism. "Jefferson Standard," *Greensboro Daily News & Record*, 8 August 1982.
32. "The Jefferson Standard," *State*, 11 August 1945.

Chapter One Sidebar: P. D. Gold

1. Mary Pleasant Daniel Gold III to Jack Bilyeu, editor, *The Jeffersonian*, 8 May 1982. Jefferson-Pilot archive.
2. "Pleasant Daniel Gold," *The Jeffersonian*, March 1965, p. 16.

Chapter Two

1. "The Jefferson Standard Becomes of Age," *The Jeffersonian*, August 1928, p. 5.
2. Amy Joyner, "Jefferson Building," *Greensboro News*

& *Record*, 16 May 1999, p. A-1

3. "A Straightforward Talk about The City Club," *The Jeffersonian*, Vol. II, No. 11, July 1924, p. 2

4. "The Jefferson Standard Life Insurance Company," *The Jeffersonian*, Vol. III, No. 10, June 1925, p. 2.

5. Ibid.

6. "Julian Price—Our President," *The Jeffersonian*, November 1928, p. 1.

7. "Review and Statement for year ending Dec. 31, 1919," *The Pilot*, March 1920, p. 2.

8. "Contempt for Small Saving," *The Pilot*, 13 January 1920, p. 3.

9. "A Brief Resume of Pilot History," pamphlet, undated, Jefferson-Pilot archive.

10. "Convention Dates January 3, 4, and 5," *The Pilot*, Vol. 10, No. 17, 2 May 1922.

11. *Greensboro Daily News*, 29 May 1971, p. D7

12. "A Brief Resume of Pilot History."

13. "A. M. Scales Portrait Dedicated," *Greensboro News and Record*, 6 February 2000, p. 2.

14. "Some Greensboro merchants are giving up credit for cash," *Greensboro Patriot*, 28 September 1898.

15. "Rotogravure Picture Section."

16. "The Creed of the McAlister Clan," *The Pilot*, July 1929, p. 3.

17. George Brown Tindall and David Emory Shi, *America* (New York: W. W. Norton, 1997), p. 835.

18. "The Jefferson Standard," pamphlet, 1956, Jefferson-Pilot archive.

19. Covington, Howard Jr. and Marion Ellis, "Making of a Giant," *News and Record*, 13 June 1993, p. E5.

20. A. W. McAlister to Mr. F. E. Cann, 8 December 1930, Jefferson-Pilot archive.

21. "Prods from the President," *The Jeffersonian*, August 1930, p. 3.

22. "General Conferences," notebook, undated, Jefferson-Pilot archive.

23. Pilot Life Insurance Company, Annual Statement, 31 December 1934.

24. Ibid.

25. Minutes of Executive Department Conference 1935-1937, 5 November 1934, Jefferson-Pilot archive.

26. "Pilot Pictorial," undated, Jefferson-Pilot archive, p. 2.

27. "Three Records Established by Pilot Life During 1937; 35th annual meeting held," *Greensboro Daily News*, 26 January 1938.

28. "History of the Pilot Life Insurance Company," pamphlet, undated, p. 3.

29. "Jefferson Standard Life Insurance Company," brochure, 1932, Jefferson-Pilot archive.

30. "President Price Submits Encouraging Statement," *Greensboro Daily News*, 25 July 1933.

31. Carl Goerch, "The Jefferson Standard," *The State*, 6 August 1938, p. 7.

32. Ibid.

33. "Letter from the President," *The Jeffersonian*, October 1939.

34. Joyner, "Jefferson Building."

35. Ibid.

36. "Broadcasting: WBGH, WBT and WBTV," pamphlet, undated, Walter Clinton Jackson Library.

37. *The Journal*, Jefferson family publication, January 1985, Jefferson-Pilot archive.

Chapter Two Sidebar: Bryan

1. Ned Cline, *Adding Value* (Asheboro, N.C.: Down Home Press, 2001).

2. Ann Rambeaut, interviewed by Richard F. Hubbard, tape recording, 9 December 2002, Write Stuff Enterprises.

Chapter Three

1. "The Jefferson Standard," *The State*, 11 August 1945, p. 17.

2. "Business of Life Insurance Companies in North Carolina for the year ending December 31, 1940," Pilot Life 1940 Annual Statement, Jefferson-Pilot archive.

3. "Trivia," *Jefferson Standard Life*, Vol. 3, No. 6, March 1941, p. 8.

4. Seth Macon, interview by Jeffrey L. Rodengen, tape recording, 18 September 2002, Write Stuff Enterprises.

5. "The Commentator," December 1977, p. 2.

6. Jim Blackburn, interview by Richard F. Hubbard, tape recording, 18 September 2002, Write Stuff Enterprises.

7. Bessie Land, interview by Richard F. Hubbard, tape recording, 18 September 2002, Write Stuff Enterprises.

8. "The Jefferson Standard," *The State*, 11 August 1945.

9. "Pilot Life Sets Records in 1944," *Greensboro News & Record*, 24 January 1945.

10. Archie Coleman, interview by Richard F. Hubbard, tape recording, 18 September 2002, Write Stuff Enterprises.

11. Ibid.

12. Randy Macon, interview by Richard F. Hubbard, tape

recording, 18 September 2002, Write Stuff Enterprises.

13. Julian Price, "Message to Shareholders," Jefferson Standard Annual Statement 1945, Jefferson-Pilot archives.

14. Bill Seawell Jr., interviewed by Richard F. Hubbard and Jeffrey L. Rodengen, tape recording, 18 September 2002, Write Stuff Enterprises.

15. Price, "Message to shareholders."

16. "Julian Price," *The Jeffersonian*, 27 October 1946.

17. "More Than 2,000 Attend Funeral for Julian Price," *Greensboro Daily News*, 28 October 1946.

18. Joe Webster Jr., interview by Richard F. Hubbard, tape recording, 4 November 2002, Write Stuff Enterprises.

19. "Julian Price," *The Jeffersonian*, 27 October 1946.

20. "Stockholders of Pilot Life Offered Big Profit on Shares," *Greensboro News*, 2 February 1945.

21. "Gate City Life Picks Officers," *Greensboro News*, undated, Jefferson-Pilot archives.

22. "The Jefferson Standard," *The State*, 11 August 1945.

23. "Jefferson Standard's First Six Months' Sales Highest in Company's History," press release, 15 July 1947.

24. "Many Big Life Insurance Firms Flourish in the State," *ESC Quarterly*, fall 1948, p. 85.

25. "Insurance Company Sets All-Time Record in '48," *Greensboro News*, 26 January 1949.

26. L. A. Crawford, "History of Pilot Life Insurance Company," March 1952.

27. Joe Freeman Sr., interview by Richard F. Hubbard, tape recording, 16 September 2002, Write Stuff Enterprises.

28. "The Jefferson Standard," undated, Jefferson-Pilot archives.

29. *Statistical Abstract of the United States*, Department of Commerce, Current Population Reports, 1970, p. 316.

30. Seth Macon, interview by Richard Hubbard, tape recording, 18 September 2002, Write Stuff Enterprises.

31. *The Jeffersonian*, June 1950, p. 3.

32. Seth Macon interview.

33. Ibid.

34. Ibid.

35. *The Communicator*, August 1968, p. 1.

36. Nancy Elkins, interview by Richard F. Hubbard, tape recording, 5 November 2002, Write Stuff Enterprises.

37. Land, interview.

38. *The Communicator*, November 1969, p. 1.

39. Pilot Life Annual Report, 1950.

40. Ibid.

41. *The State*, 19 December 1953, p. 6.

42. Ibid.

43. Pilot Life Annual Report, 1954.

44. *Life with Pilot*, Feb. 1960, p. 6.

45. Roger Soles, interview by Jeffrey L. Rodengen, tape recording, 2 October 2002, Write Stuff Enterprises.

46. Jefferson Standard Annual Report, 1951.

47. Jack Warmath, interview by Richard F. Hubbard, tape recording, 29 October 2002, Write Stuff Enterprises.

48. Ibid.

49. Jefferson Standard Annual Report, 1951.

50. Ibid, p. 2.

51. Ibid.

52. Robert H. Koonts, interview by Richard F. Hubbard, tape recording, 6 November 2002, Write Stuff Enterprises.

53. Jefferson Standard Annual Report, 1959, p. 1.

54. *The Jeffersonian*, June 1967, p. 4.

55. *Life with Pilot*, February 1966, p. 16.

56. *Statistical Abstract of the United States*, Department of Commerce, Bureau of the Census, Current Population Reports, 1949–2000.

57. *Statistical Abstract of the United States*, Department of Commerce, 1980, p. 548.

58. Dick Andrews, interview by Richard F. Hubbard, tape recording, 26 September 2002, Write Stuff Enterprises.

59. Ibid.

60. Ibid.

61. Ibid.

62. Bette B. Johnson, interview by Richard F. Hubbard, tape recording, 18 September 2002, Write Stuff Enterprises.

63. Craig McIntosh, interview by Richard F. Hubbard, tape recording, 17 September 2002, Write Stuff Enterprises.

64. Seth Macon, "The Agency Department: How It Grew – 1907-1970," *The Jeffersonian*, May 1982, pp. 6–8.

65. Ibid.

66. Seth C. Macon, "The Vital Link: A Guided Tour of the Agency Department—With Commentary," *The Jeffersonian*, April 1982, pp. 6–9.

67. Ben Tabor, interview by Richard F. Hubbard, tape recording, 5 May 2001, Write Stuff Enterprises.

68. Jefferson Standard Annual Report, 1960; Pilot Life Annual Report, 1960.
69. Pilot Life Annual Report, 1965.
70. Jefferson Standard Annual Report, 1965.
71. *The Jeffersonian*, June 1967, p. 4.

Chapter Three Sidebar: Holderness

1. *The Jeffersonian*, June 1967, p. 4.
2. Ibid.

Chapter Three Sidebar: Miss Mary

1. Bill Seawell Jr., interviewed by Richard F. Hubbard, tape recording, 18 September 2002, Write Stuff Enterprises.

Chapter Three Sidebar: Communications

1. Rod Hackney, "WBIG goes off the Air," *Greensboro News and Record*, 21 November 1986.
2. Ned Cline, "Adding Value."
3. Ibid.
4. "Award Lauds Talents of Old-Time Band," by Joe Depriest, *The Charlotte Observer*, March 22, 2002, Page 1L, Gaston Section.
5. "WBT's Pilot Briarhopper Family Album," pamphlet, 1949, Jefferson-Pilot archive.
6. Justin Catanoso, "Bryan Excelled in Business and Benevolence," *Greensboro News and Record*, 27 April 1995, p. A-7.
7. "Broadcasting: WBGH, WBT and WBTV."

Chapter Four

1. *The Jeffersonian*, August 1968, pp. 8–9.

2. Ibid.
3. Koonts, interview.
4. Coleman, interview.
5. Andrews, interview.
6. "Rufus White: Retiring," pamphlet, undated, Jefferson-Pilot archive.
7. Louis Stephens, interview by Richard F. Hubbard, tape recording, 22 October 2002, Write Stuff Enterprises.
8. Seth Macon, interview.
9. Warmath, interview.
10. Soles, interview.
11. Ibid.
12. John Still, interview by Jeffrey L. Rodengen, tape recording, 16 September 2002, Write Stuff Enterprises.
13. Dorothy Austell, interview by Richard F. Hubbard, tape recording, 19 November 2002, Write Stuff Enterprises.
14. Molly Walls, interview by Richard F. Hubbard, tape recording, 25 October 2002, Write Stuff Enterprises.
15. Loretta Courson, interview by Richard F. Hubbard, tape recording, 8 November 2002, Write Stuff Enterprises.
16. Ibid.
17. *The Jeffersonian*, August 1982, p. 8.
18. John Ingram, interview by Jeffrey L. Rodengen, tape recording, 18 September 2002, Write Stuff Enterprises.
19. Ibid.
20. Ibid.
21. Jefferson Standard Annual Reports, 1970, 1975, and 1980.
22. Lloyd Gordon, interview by Richard F. Hubbard, tape recording, 16 September 2002, Write Stuff Enterprises.
23. John Shreves, interview by Richard F. Hubbard, tape recording, 24 October 2002, Write Stuff Enterprises.

24. Ed Hull, interviewed by Richard F. Hubbard, tape recording, 12 December 2002, Write Stuff Enterprises.
25. Bert East, interview by Richard F. Hubbard, tape recording, 18 September 2002, Write Stuff Enterprises.
26. Sam Elkins, interview by Richard F. Hubbard, tape recording, 31 October 2002, Write Stuff Enterprises.
27. Mary Onn Parham, interview by Richard F. Hubbard, tape recording, 17 September 2002, Write Stuff Enterprises.
28. Andrews, interview.
29. Frank Starr, interview by Richard F. Hubbard, tape recording, 17 September 2002, Write Stuff Enterprises.
30. Pilot Life 75th anniversary brochure, 1 July 1978, Jefferson-Pilot archive.
31. Bob Martin, interview by Richard F. Hubbard, tape recording, 23 October 2002, Write Stuff Enterprises.
32. *The Pilot*, September 1986, pp. 1–4.
33. Pilot Life 75th anniversary brochure.
34. Ibid.
35. Still, interview.

Chapter Four Sidebar: Roger Soles

1. *JP Life Magazine*, February 1993, pp. 1–5.

Chapter Five

1. *The Jeffersonian*, August 1982, p. 10.
2. Ibid.
3. Pilot Life Annual Report, 1981, pp. 3–9.
4. Pilot Life Annual Report, 1982, p. 1.

5. Jefferson-Pilot 4th Quarter Report, 1985, p. 1.
6. *JP Life Magazine*, February 1991, pp. 8–9.
7. Hull, interview.
8. Ibid.
9. Ibid.
10. Ibid.
11. Clarke Brown, interview by Richard F. Hubbard, tape recording, 11 November 2002, Write Stuff Enterprises.
12. Jefferson-Pilot 4th Quarter Report, 9 February 1987, p. 1.
13. Jack Scism, *Greensboro News & Record*, 26 August 1986.
14. *Life with Pilot*, August 1986, p. 1.
15. Koonts, interview.
16. *The Journal*, October 1986, p. 1.
17. *Inside JP*, March 1988, pp. 1–2.
18. Joe Wheeler, interview by Richard F. Hubbard, tape recording, 18 September 2002, Write Stuff Enterprises.
19. Ralph Seigler, interview by Richard F. Hubbard, tape recording, 4 November 2002, Write Stuff Enterprises.
20. Randy Macon, interview.
21. Nancy Elkins, interview.
22. East, interview.
23. "Looking Back, Moving Forward," *The Pilot*, September 1986, pp. 4–6.
24. Sam Elkins, interview.
25. Nancy Elkins, interview.
26. Ibid.
27. Ibid.
28. Jefferson-Pilot Annual Report, 1990, pp. 1–2.
29. *JP Life Magazine*, February 1991, pp. 8–9.
30. Jefferson-Pilot Annual Report, 1990.
31. Jack Scism, *Greensboro News & Record*, 26 August 1986.
32. Jefferson-Pilot Annual Report, 1990, p. 2.
33. Soles, interview.
34. *JP Life*, February 1993, p. 3.
35. Soles, interview.

Chapter Six

1. Jim Melvin, interview by Jeffrey L. Rodengen, tape recording, 17 September 2002, Write Stuff Enterprises.
2. "Jefferson-Pilot: The Vision to Power Your Dreams," pamphlet, March 1993, Jefferson-Pilot archive.
3. *Business: North Carolina*, August 1994, pp. 22–28.
4. Melvin, interview.
5. Ken Mlekush, interview by Jeffrey L. Rodengen, tape recording, 17 September 2002, Write Stuff Enterprises.
6. Hoyt Phillips, interview by Jeffrey L. Rodengen, tape recording, 16 September 2002, Write Stuff Enterprises.
7. Mlekush, interview.
8. Ingram, interview.
9. Jefferson-Pilot Annual Report, 1990, pp. 3, 6, and 49.
10. Bill Pickering, interview by Richard F. Hubbard, tape recording, 31 October 2002, Write Stuff Enterprises.
11. David Stonecipher, interview by Jeffrey L. Rodengen, tape recording, 17 September 2002, Write Stuff Enterprises.
12. Mlekush, interview.
13. Martin, interview.
14. Jefferson-Pilot Annual Report, 1994, p. 10.
15. Mark Konen, interview by Richard F. Hubbard, tape recording, 5 November 2002, Write Stuff Enterprises.
16. Ibid.
17. Dennis Glass, interview by Jeffrey L. Rodengen, tape recording, 17 September 2002, Write Stuff Enterprises.
18. Jefferson-Pilot Annual Report, 1993.
19. Jefferson-Pilot Annual Report, 1996, p. 46.
20. Ibid.
21. Mlekush, interview.
22. Ibid.
23. *Insight*, vol. 12, no. 1, spring/summer 1997, Chubb Life Insurance Company, p. 6.
24. John Hopkins, interview by Richard F. Hubbard, tape recording, 4 November 2002, Write Stuff Enterprises.
25. Ron Angarella, interview by Jeffrey L. Rodengen, tape recording, 2 October 2002, Write Stuff Enterprises.
26. Mlekush, interview.
27. Terry Stone, interview by Jeffrey L. Rodengen, tape recording, 17 December 2002, Write Stuff Enterprises.
28. *Insight*, vol. 12, no. 1, spring/summer 1997, Chubb Life Insurance Company, p. 6.
29. Angarella, interview.
30. Chuck Cornelio, interview by Richard F. Hubbard, tape recording, 2 October 2002, Write Stuff Enterprises.
31. Brown, interview.
32. Hull, interview.
33. Ibid.
34. "From the Office of the Chief Executive Officer," undated press release, Jefferson-Pilot archives.
35. Ann Dowd, interview by Jeffrey L. Rodengen, tape recording, 18 September 2002, Write Stuff Enterprises.
36. Bob Bates, interview by Jeffrey L. Rodengen, tape recording, 14 October 2002, Write Stuff Enterprises.
37. Ibid.

38. Phillips, interview.
39. Bates, interview.
40. Mlekush, interview.
41. JP press release, 30 December, 1999.
42. Jefferson-Pilot Summary Annual Report, 2000, p. 5.
43. "JPF Premier Partnering Strategy," *Bylines*, winter 2001.
44. Stone, interview.
45. Internal Jefferson-Pilot memorandum, 1 July 2002.
46. Stonecipher, interview.
47. Jefferson-Pilot press release, 30 August 2001, Jefferson-Pilot archive.
48. Jefferson-Pilot press release, 19 February 2002, Jefferson-Pilot archive.
49. Jefferson-Pilot press release, 15 March 2001, Jefferson-Pilot archive.
50. Ibid.
51. Mlekush, interview.
52. Stonecipher, interview.
53. Phillips, interview.
54. Mlekush, interview.
55. "Talking Performance with Warren May," *Bylines*, 2003, Jefferson-Pilot archive.
56. Doug Campbell, "Dennis Glass has his finger on the trigger, and it's only a matter of time before he pulls again," *Greensboro News & Record*, 7 March 1999.
57. "Talking Performance with Dennis Glass," *Bylines*, 2003, Jefferson-Pilot Archive.
58. "Manufacturing," *Bylines*, winter 2001.
59. Cornelio, interview.
60. Austell, interview.
61. Stonecipher, interview.

Chapter Six Sidebar: Stonecipher

1. *Business: North Carolina*, August 1994, p. 25.
2. *JP Life Magazine*, March 1993, p. 2.

Chapter Six Sidebar: Premiere Partner

1. Stoncipher, interview.
2. Sam Cornwell, interview by Richard F. Hubbard, tape recording, 11 November 2002, Write Stuff Enterprises.
3. Ron Agel, interview by Richard L. Hubbard, tape recording, 19 November 2002, Write Stuff Enterprises.
4. Guy Hatcher, interview by Richard F. Hubbard, tape recording, 19 November 2002, Write Stuff Enterprises.
5. Pickering, interview.
6. Dave Misiak, interview by Richard F. Hubbard, tape recording, 4 November 2002, Write Stuff Enterprises.
7. Michael Lyman, interview by Richard F. Hubbard, tape recording, 11 November 2002, Write Stuff Enterprises.
8. Norm Feinstein, interview by Richard F. Hubbard, tape recording, 11 November 2002, Write Stuff Enterprises.
9. J. J. Field, interview by Richard F. Hubbard, tape recording, 19 November 2002, Write Stuff Enterprises.
10. Courson, interview.
11. Bernie Bernstein, interview by Richard F. Hubbard, tape recording, 20 November 2002, Write Stuff Enterprises.

INDEX

Page numbers in italics indicate photographs.

A

ABGA (Agency Building General Agent system), 136
abstainer's agreement, *18*
Accident and Health Department, 79
acquisitions and mergers. *See also* radio and TV stations
Alexander Hamilton Life, 129, 130
Chubb Life Insurance Co., 129–131, *131*
formation of Jefferson-Pilot Life Insurance Co., 111, 113
Guarantee Life Companies, 133–136, *135*
Jefferson buys Pilot Life, 50, *51*, 52
Jefferson Standard/Greensboro Life Insurance Co., 31–32
Jefferson Standard/Security Life and Annuity Co., 32–33
Kentucky Central Life, 128–129, 130
Pilot Life and Gate City Life, 68, 70–71, *71*
acquisition strategy, 122, 126, 128, 140–141
advertising, *53*, 95
Jefferson-Pilot, 113, 140
and Jefferson-Pilot Teleproductions, 100–101
Jefferson Standard Life Insurance Co., *24*, 28, 30, *61*, 71
Pilot Life, 85, 87, *102*, 103
Agel, Ron, 138
Alexander Hamilton Life, 129, 130
alliances, 140
Allstate, 140
American Council of Life Insurance, 108
American Temperance Life Insurance Co., 12
Andrews, Dick, 13–14, 85, 95, 100, *101*, 103, 113
Andrews, W. H., 126
Angarella, Ron, 130

Atlantic Coast Conference, *101*, 103, 108, *110*
Austell, Dorothy, 142–143

B

Banc of America Investment Services, 140
Barton, Harry, 42
basketball sponsorship, 85, 103, 108, *110*
Bates, Bob, 134, *134*, 135
Benefit Partners, 134
Bernstein, Bernie, 139
billion dollar milestone, Jefferson Standard, 80, *80, 82*
Blackburn, Jim, 64
Blackwell, Bill, *120*, 131
bonds, *14, 15*
Borden, Edwin B., *141*
Briarhoppers, 87
Brooks, Aubrey Lee, 33
Brown, Clarke, 101, 111, 132
Brown, Joseph Gill, 28
Bryan, Joseph, Jr., 60
Bryan, Joseph M., 60, *60*, 61, 67, 75, 86–87, 101, 131
Bryan, Kathleen Price, 60, 61, 68
Bryan, Kay and Nancy, 60

C

calendars, *35, 65*, 70
Carolina Mutual Life Insurance Co., 38
Carroll, Dudley, 104
Carter, Jimmy, *128*
Carter, Maybelle, 87
Carter, Rosalyn, *128*
Carter, Sara, 87
Cavanaugh, George, 80, 96, 98
CBS, 86
Charlotte Observer, 87
Chartered Life Underwriter, 98
Chatfield, H. G., 28

Chubb Life Insurance Co., 129–131, *131*
Citizens National Bank, 28
City Club, 38
Cole, Grady, 86
Coleman, Archie, 65–66, 95
College Football Association, 108
computer systems, *94*, 94–95, *95*
Cornelio, Chuck, 130, 131, 142
Cornwell, Sam, 138
corporate culture, 142–143
Courson, Loretta, 97, 99, 139
Cridland, R. B., 42
Crutchfield, Charles, 87
Cunningham, William H., *140*

D, E, F

DAN (District Agency Network), 126
Daniels, Josephus, 26
divestitures, 126
Dowd, Ann, 134

East, Bert, 115
Elkins, Nancy, 76, 115, 116
Elkins, Sam, 102, 115
ESPN, 108
exercise breaks, 16–18, *17*

Fee, Tom, 124
Feinstein, Norm, 139
Ferguson, C. Randolph, *120*
Field, J. J., 139
First Alexander Hamilton Life Insurance Co., 129
flu epidemic, 22, 35
football sponsorships, 108
Fortune 500, 142
Fortune, Adelaide, 74
Fortune, Mrs. John C, 56
Fox Film Co., 27
Freeman, Joe, Jr., 72
Freeman, Joe, Sr., 70, 72

G

Garinger, Elmer, 79
Gate City Life Insurance Co., 58, 68, 70, 70–71, *71*
George Washington Fire Insurance Co., 13, 49
Glass, Dennis, *120*, 124, 128, 141, 142, *143*
Goerch, Carl, 59
Gold, Charles, 25, 27, 52, *52*
Gold, John, 27
Gold, P. D., 25, 27, *27*, 31, 33, 91
golf, 21, *21*, 53
Gordon, Lloyd, 100
Great Depression, 49, 56
Green, Emry C., *52*, 52–56, 70
Greensboro Country Club, 21
Greensboro Daily News, 87, 91
Greensboro Daily Record, 61
Greensboro Fire Insurance Co., 13, 49
Greensboro Life Insurance Co., *29*, 31–32, 37
Greensboro National Bank, 49
Greensboro News Co., 86
Greensboro News & Record, 67, 113, 116, 119
Greer, Robert G, *141*
Grimsley, George A., 26, 33, *33*
group insurance, 70, 72, *72*, 111, 126, 133–134
Guarantee Life Companies, 133–136, *135*
Guilford National Bank, 49

H

Habitat for Humanity, *128*
Hartman, Charles C., 36
Hatcher, Guy, 138
headquarters buildings
    Chubb Life, *131*
    Guarantee Life Companies, *135*
    Jefferson-Pilot building, *103*, *112*, 113–114, *117*
    Jefferson Standard building, *34*, 36, *36*, 38, *55*, *78*, *111*, 113
    Pilot Life Insurance Co. (*see* Sedgefield)
    Southern Loan & Trust, *12–13*
Health and Conservation Department, 21
health insurance, 111, 126
Heidrick & Struggles, 121
Henderson, George W., III, *141*
Highland Capital, 140
Holderness, George A., 25, 74, 75
Holderness, Howard "Chick," *74*
    elected president of Jefferson Standard, 75–76
    leadership, 82–83
    original stockholder, 25
    profile of, 74
    retirement, 90–91, *91*
Holderness & Company Investments, 75
holding company, formation of, 93–94
Home Services division, 103, 126
Hopkins, John D., *120*, 122, *122*, 129–130
hospitalization insurance, 79

Household International, 129
Hudgins, B. Edward, 82, 94, 96
Hull, Ed, 101, 108, 110, 132

IMO Channel, 125, *127*
Industrial Division, 103, 126
Industrial Weekly Premium Department, 72
Ingram, John, 100, 125
Integon Life Insurance Corp., 33
Intermediate Division, 39–40
Inter-Ocean Casualty Co., 49
Irving Park, *42*

James, Carl, *101*
Jefferson-Pilot building, *103*, *112*, 113–114, *117*
Jefferson-Pilot Choraliers, 116
Jefferson-Pilot Communications, 61, *86*, 86–87, 100–102, 108–111, 131–133, 137
Jefferson-Pilot Corp.
    formation of holding company, 93–94, 100
Jefferson-Pilot Life Insurance Co., 111, 113
Jefferson-Pilot Sports, 100–101, 108–111, 132–133, *133*
Jefferson-Pilot Teleproductions. *See* Jefferson-Pilot Sports
Jefferson Standard building, *34*, 36, *36*, 38, *55*, *78*, *111*, 113
Jefferson Standard Club, 38, *54*, 66, *66*
Jefferson Standard Life Insurance Co.
    acquisition of Pilot Life, 50–52, *51*
    advertising, *24*, 28, 30, *61*, 71
    billion dollar milestone, 80, 82
    50th anniversary, *84*
    founding of, 25–26
    insurance policies, *26*
    investments, 80–81
    marketing, *29*
    office staff, *58*
    and Pilot Life, 46, 64
    postwar growth, 71–72
    Puerto Rico office, *73*
    and Roger Soles, 97–100
    World War II, 64–65
Johnson, Bette B., 88
Jorgensen, Wallace, 108
J-P Publications, 97
JPSC (Jefferson Pilot Securities Corp.), 130

K, L, M

Kentucky Central Life, 128–129, 130
King & Spalding, 122
Kirby, Fred, 87
Knickerbockers Trust Co., 28
Kodak Road to Olympic Gold, 132–133
Konen, Mark, 124, 128
Koonts, Robert, 82, 94, 113, 124

Land, Bessie, 65, 76
Laxtton, Fred N., 86
legal department, 82

Liberty Bonds, 22
Life of Georgia, 123, 124
Lindley, Jack, 75
Ljung, Karl, 88–90, *91*, 96
logos
    Jefferson-Pilot, *93*, *121*, 133–136
    Jefferson Standard, 28, *28*
    Pilot Life Insurance Co., *41*, 85, *107*
    Southern Life & Trust, *11*, 14
Long, Lydia Valk, *141*
Lyman, Michael, 139

Macon, Randy, 66, 114
Macon, Seth, 64, 75, 89, 96–97
Martin, Bob, 103–104, 126
Matthews, Mrs. E. T., 56
May, Warren H., 141, *142*
McAlister, Alexander Carey, 16
McAlister, A. W., *19*, *46*
    business principles, 16–19, 43, 46, 47, *47*
    career advancement, 14, 16
    community service, 19, 21
    health advocacy, 16–18
    retirement of, 52
McAlister, Vaughn, & Scales General Agency, 40
McAlister Clan, 43, 46, 47, *47*
McAlister Underwriters, 13
McKinsey & Co., 93, 136
Medicare, 85, 88
Melvin, Jim, 121, 124, *140*
mergers. *See* acquisitions and mergers
Misiak, Dave, 139
Mlekush, Kenneth C., *120*, 124, *140*
    and acquisitions, 129, 135, 141
    business strategy, 126
    joins Jefferson-Pilot, 124, 125
    named vice chairman, 141
    and Premier Partners program, 136
Moving Picture Health Car, 22
Mr. 4%, *90*
Myers, Albert G., 25, *91*

N, O, P

NASCAR, 110
National Drama Corp., 27
National Service Life Insurance, 71
Nelson, Wayne, 61
newspaper market, 97
New York Stock Exchange, 100, 122
North Carolina Broadcasting Co., 61
North Carolina Business Hall of Fame, 60

O'Brian, Pat, 132
office staff
    Jefferson Standard, *42*, *50*
    Pilot Life, 40–41, *83*, *94*
Olympic Games, Summer 1996, 132–133, *133*
Ordinary Health and Accident Division, 39

Parham, Mary Onn, 103
Parker, J., 28
Parsons, Don, 122
Parsons, Louise Price, 122
Payne, William Porter, *141*

Paysour, Conrad, 91
Perkins, A. R., 58
Phillips, Hoyt, 124, 125, 135, 141
Phoenix Gazette, 61
Pickering, Bill, 125, 138–139
Pilot Fire Insurance Co., 13, *21*, 49
Pilot Life Insurance Co. *See also*
        Southern Life & Trust Co.
    acquired by Jefferson Standard,
        50–52, *51*
    advertising, 85, 87, *102*, 103
    Gate City merger, 68, 70–71, *71*,
        72
    marketing, *49*
    naming of, 40
    North Carolina, contributions to,
        79
    office staff, *39*, 40–41
    postwar growth, 72
    stock buyback, 64
    surpasses Jefferson Standard, 83,
        85
    50th anniversary, *83*
    World War II, *63*, *64*, 64–65
Pilot Mountain, *11*, 14, *20*, 21, *48*
Pittard, Patrick, *140*
polio epidemic, 86
Poole, Bob, 86, 100
Premier Partner program, *136*,
        136–137, *138*, 138–139,
        139
President's Club, 38
preventive medicine, *23*
Price, Ethel Clay, *37*, *57*, 68, *69*
Price, Julian, *57*, *58*, *67*, *69*
    business acumen, 35
    career advancement, 33
    and *Charlotte Observer*, 87
    death of, 68
    and Greensboro Life Insurance
        Co., 31
    media investment, 61
    profile of, 37
    retirement, 66–68
    succession plan, 58
Price, Kathleen. *See* Bryan, Kathleen
        Price
Price, Ralph, 58, *67*, 68, 75–76
proxy fight, 122
Puerto Rico, *73*

R, S

radio and TV stations, 61, 86,
        100–102, 109, *109*, 111. *See
        also* Jefferson-Pilot
        Communications
Rambeaut, Ann, 60
Reconstruction Finance Corp., 49
reorganization, 93–97
Retton, Mary Lou, 132
Ridge, Edney, 86
Russell, Donald S. Jr., *141*

"Sail with the Pilot" theme song, 85, *88*
sales agents
    ABGA (formerly Career Channel),
        125–126, 136
    IMO Channel, 125, *127*
    Jefferson Standard, 31, 38, *50*,
        90, *90*, *92*, 136–137
    Premier Partner program,
        136–137, *138*, 138–139, *139*
    Stonecipher strategy, 125–126,
        136–137
    women, 56
Salute Freedom Fireworks, *119*
Sarbanes-Oxley legislation, 122
scholastic accident insurance, 72, 79
schoolchildren, marketing to. *see*
        youth market
Scism, Jack, 67, 113
Seawell, Bill, II, 126
Seawell, Bill, Jr., 66–67, 81
Security Life and Annuity Co., *29*,
        32–33
Security Life and Trust, 33, 63
Security National Bank, 49
Sedgefield, *40–41*, *62*, *96*, *114*, *115*
    closing of, 113–115
    development of, 41–43, *44–45*
    expansion of, 79
    Sedgefield Inn, 42, *43*, 64
Seigler, Ralph, 107, 114
Seigler, Roger, 126
Shreves, John, 100, 132
Smith, Albert Lee, 38
Social Security, 71–72
Soles, Jan, *99*
Soles, Majelle, *99*
Soles, Melanie, *99*
Soles, Roger, *84*, *98*, *99*, *118*
    leadership, 97–100
    and Seth Macon, 96–97
    named president, 91
    and reorganziation, 93, 111, 113
    retirement, 115, 119
    succession following, 124
Soles, William, *99*
Southeastern Broadcasting, 86–87
Southeastern Conference, 108, *110*
Southern Life & Trust Co., 14, *32*
Southern Loan & Trust Co., *10*, *11*,
        12–13, 12–16
Southern Real Estate Co., 14, 42
Southern Stock Fire Insurance Co.,
        13, 16
Spencer, Lance, 86
Spencer, Maynard, 86
Spilman, Robert, 122
sports sponsorships, 85, 103, 108,
        110, *110*
Stafford, O. F., 77, *83*
    leadership, 70, 76, 79, 82
    profile of, 76
    retirement, 95
Starr, Frank, 103, 107

Stephens, Louis, 96, *101*, 102, *103*,
        104–105, 107, 115
Still, John, 97, 105
Stone, Terry, 130, *132*, 137, 141
Stonecipher, David, *120*, *123*, *140*
    and acquisitions, 126–131,
        133–136, 140–141
    joins Jefferson-Pilot, 119, 121–122
    and management team, 124–125
    and marketing strategy, 125–126,
        138–139
    profile, 123
    and proxy fight, 122
Stonecipher, Nancy, 123
Strug, Kerri, 133
subsidiaries, 93–94. *See also* radio and
        TV stations; individual
        companies

T, U, V

Tabor, Ben L., 89–90
Taylor, Miss Mary, *58*, 81, *81*
technology, *94*, 94–95, *95*
Tice, Jim, 99
Tulsa Tribune, 61
TV stations. *See* radio and TV stations

universal life insurance, 105, 137
U.S. Women's Gymnastics Team,
        132–133, *133*

Vanguard Group, 140
Van Lindley, John, 75
Vaughn, Robert Galloway, 10
Vaughn & Scales, *21*
VUL (variable universal life), 129

W, Y, Z

Walls, Carmage, 97
Walls, Molly, 97
Warmath, Jack, 80–81, 97, 124
WBIG, 61, 86, *109*
Webster, Joe Jr., 68
Weekly Premium Department, 40
W. H. Andrews Jr. Award, 126, 139
Wharton, E. P., 12, 14
Wheeler, Joe, 114
White, Bill, 126
White, M. A. "Jack," 67
White, Rufus, 96, *96*
World War I, 22
World War II, 59, *63*, *64*, 64–65, 71
Worth, John M., 12
Worth, Thomas C., 12
Worth-Wharton Real Estate &
        Investment Co., *12–13*, 12–14

Yelton, E. Jay, *120*, 124
youth market, 72, 79, 85, *88*, 102

Zantsinger, Borie and Madary, 42